MANY PATHS TO GOD

Periodically throughout history great teachers and prophets have brought messages of love and wisdom to peoples of different cultures and countries. From their lives and teachings the great religions of the world have developed, each having its own revered writings and beliefs. While their external details may vary, there are many points of similarity in their essential concepts, and in their ethical and moral teachings they are in remarkable agreement.

In this book Ruby L. Radford presents in simple and beautiful form the basic ideas of twelve living religions and describes many of their parallel teachings. In addition to the major world faiths of Hinduism, Buddhism, Judaism, Christianity, and Islam, there are sections on the religions of China (Taoism and Confucianism) and Japan (Shintoism), and the smaller but nonetheless active faiths of Zoroastrianism, Jainism, and Sikhism — found mainly in India and Pakistan — and the newest religion, Baha'i. The book is handsomely and richly illustrated with actual photographs of temples and followers of the various faiths. It is a valuable introduction to the subject of comparative religion for young adults and helpful to providing a deeper appreciation of the religions of others.

Ruby L. Radford has written more than fifty books for children and young adults, as well as many short stories and serials. In 1969 she was voted "Author of the Year" by the Dixie Council of Authors and Journalists.

Books by Ruby L. Radford:

THE ENCHANTED HILL (A Quest Book for Children)
JULIETTE LOW: GIRL SCOUT FOUNDER
PRELUDE TO FAME
DWIGHT D. EISENHOWER
ROSE-COLORED GLASSES (A Quest Book for Children)

and 45 other books for children and young adults

MANY PATHS TO GOD

by

RUBY L. RADFORD

A QUEST BOOK for Young Adults
Published under a grant from The Kern Foundation

THE THEOSOPHICAL PUBLISHING HOUSE
Wheaton, Illinois, U.S.A.
Madras, India / London, England

SR 3/73

The Theosophical Publishing House, Wheaton, Illinois, is a department of
The Theosophical Society in America.

Library of Congress Catalog Card Number: 77-122431
ISBN: 0-8356-0408-X

Manufactured in the United States of America

To

DOROTHY LEHMAN SUMERAU

"However men approach Me, even so do I welcome
  them, for the paths men take from every side are Mine."

— *Bhagavad-Gita*

"God sends his teachers unto every age,
  To every clime, and every race of men,
  With revelations fitted to their growth
  And shape of mind, nor gives the realm of Truth
  Into the selfish rule of one sole race:
  Therefore each form of worship that hath swayed
  The life of man, and given it to grasp
  The master key of knowledge, reverence
  Infolds some germs of goodness and of right; . . ."

— From *Rhoecus* by James Russell Lowell

Acknowledgments

The author is grateful to the Kern Foundation for the Fellowship which made the writing of this book possible. Also I wish to express my gratitude to many people who helped in various ways during the preparation of this manuscript, especially my editor, Helen Zahara, for her patience and wise guidance in the selection of material and the editing of the book. Seetha Neelakantan of the Adyar Library, Madras, India, has rendered great assistance through her knowledge of the Eastern religions, and especially for her careful editing of the chapter on Hinduism. Thanks are also due to Virginia Hanson, editor of *The American Theosophist,* Dorothy Lehman Sumerau, Josie A. Radford, Florice Tanner, and Rose Wilson, a young adult, for reading and editorial assistance. I am also grateful to Rabbi Norman Goldberg and Clarence Cohen, who checked the accuracy of my chapter on Judaism, and to Mazuda Assisi of Afghanistan for editing my chapter on Islam.

The Temple of Understanding in Washington, D.C., cooperated by putting me in touch with the representatives of various Eastern countries, who have assisted me through letters, booklets, and other information: D. Piyananda on Buddhism; Sadguru Keshavadas on Hinduism; Professor Wen Yen Tsao of Milligan College on Confucianism; and Dr. A. H. Abdel Kader of the Islamic Center in Washington, D.C. Especial thanks are also due to the staff of the Augusta-Richmond County Library, to Elithe Nisewanger of the Theosophical Society in Madras, India, and to Helen Loenholdt of the Theosophical Library in Wheaton, Illinois, for supplying me with many books on world religions.

Ruby L. Radford

Contents

Illustrations

Chapter I

In the Beginning

In order to appreciate and understand the significance of the great religions of the world, we must realize that each has been a part of a Divine Plan for the gradual development and spiritual unfoldment of humanity. In the grand panorama of man's slowly awakening consciousness, each religion has played its part in expanding his spiritual nature.

As teachers came age after age to help men understand that they could not break the divine, unchangeable laws of life without suffering, each gave a message that was suited to the stage of man's evolutionary progress. Looking back from the twentieth century, some of the rituals and ceremonies may indeed seem primitive to us, but each served its purpose in teaching people lessons at a particular time in the development of the world.

In the Judeo-Christian Bible we read that God breathed into man the breath of life and man became a living soul. This probably refers to the time when animal-like man began to be aware that there was an over-all power greater than himself, whose rules of life he must either obey or else suffer the consequences, so the

1

spark of divinity which had been breathed into each human being began to flicker dimly, and in the ages ahead it may become a glowing flame to give light to other souls who need help.

Many names have been given to this Creator; some have used the term *God,* Jehovah, Brahma, Allah, or the Great Spirit. As mankind started the long climb toward God, some were lazy or indifferent and suffered much when the divine laws were broken; others learned their lessons easily and so forged ahead. These became leaders of humanity, teachers, rulers, warriors, poets, and priests.

As the ages passed and the world became more densely populated, every civilization produced its prophets and teachers, around whom developed different forms of religion; but the essential truths at the core of most is the Fatherhood of God and the Brotherhood of Man. Each religion developed its own form of instruction and ways of worship suited to the needs of humanity at the time. The founders or teachers of these religions have been many; among them have been Zoroaster, Moses, Isaiah, Krishna, Gautama, Mahavira, Mohammed, Lao-tse, Confucius, Jesus Christ, and Baha'u'llah. They are indeed a great spiritual hierarchy dedicated to the service of humanity.

In the dawn of man's spiritual awakening, however, he had no knowledge of a God of love. He was haunted by fears. Lightning and thunder made him cringe fearful of some over-all power. Animals and reptiles of the jungle threatened his life. He believed that floods, storms, and famines were punishment from gods he had offended.

Families clung together for protection against their common enemies and gradually learned to cooperate and live at peace among themselves. Eventually tribes cooperated for the common good, and the first simple lessons of brotherhood were learned. The needs of these primitive people were very few; food, skins of animals for clothes in colder climates, and the craving for family life and human companionship.

Wherever people were scattered about the globe they tried to understand more about the over-all power that seemed to rule their lives. Each tribe or clan formed its own ideas about the nature of the one Creator, and man's relation to him and to each other. Some worshiped minor gods and feared to offend them,

2

so men tried to appease the anger of the gods with blood sacrifices and ceremonies.

Spiritism

One of the earliest forms of religion was probably Spiritism. This is the primitive belief, still held among some isolated tribes, that rocks, trees, mountains, and streams have spirits that can help or harm a person. Animals, too, were supposed to be possessed of these spirits. When a savage killed an animal for food he apologized to the spirit he had freed. But he felt when he ate the flesh of an elephant that he gained its strength, and that he became fleet of foot from eating deer meat.

In the caves of Switzerland and Germany relics have been found that are evidence of sacrificial rites to win the good will of the cave bear. These date back 180,000 years to stone-age man. In America there were rites related to the salmon, which Indians caught in great numbers and dried for winter food.

Today members of the Ife cult in Africa take their newly-born children to the witch doctor to find out which spirits they must worship. The priest casts some fruit kernels or small rocks on the ground. Studying the way they fall, he tells the parents which spirit will watch over the child. The young are taught what not to do to keep from offending these spirits.

In this way taboos have developed. Some of these gradually became laws of the tribes, and so the people learned to obey laws though many were based on ignorance.

In the isolated mountains of Thailand there are tribes that still believe in the power of the spirits for good or evil. If a house is to be built, sacrifices must be made to the spirits. Two pigs may be cooked as a feast for the workers. A dog or chicken may be offered to the spirits that guard over the house.

In the spring when rice is to be planted, a fowl or an animal is sacrificed by the owner of the field. The priest examines the vital organs to tell if the field will produce a good crop. If the signs are unfavorable, the farmer will select another field.

Tribes like these, still living in isolation, give us an idea about the earliest religions of humanity. Explorers and missionaries have brought back reports of how such primitive people worship.

The Indians of North America believed spirits were in the

thunder. The Cherokees called these spirits *Ani-Hyun-tik-walsaki,* which meant the Thunderers. The rainbow was called, "the mantle of the thunder-god." When he wanted to descend he let down a bright end of his many-colored mantle to touch the earth. However, Indian children were taught not to point at the rainbow for fear their fingers would wither.

The Zuni Indians of the southwest called their gods Kachines. One of the ancient rituals, still practiced today, is the rain dance. As the Zunis depended on corn for their main food, they asked for help from the rain spirits every spring when they planted corn in the arid soil.

The priest or medicine man led the dancers into a cleared area. The participants performed a precise ritual dance, each movement of which had a special significance. Except for the medicine man, every dancer wore a Kachina mask. His body and arms were painted in brilliant designs. He wore a tunic, sash, and moccasins, with small bells around his ankles and knees. In his left hand each carried a gourd filled with rocks or kernels, which he rattled as he danced. Instead of a gourd, the medicine man carried a basket filled with corn meal to represent seed. He scattered this in the path of the dancers in imitation of planting corn.

As they stamped to the rhythm of drum beats, the dancers shook their rattles. Every step and turn was made to an exact pattern. The medicine man led them to face north, east, south, and west. When rain was badly needed these dances would go on through the night. Watchers clapped and shouted to the rhythm of the drums, the rattling of gourds, and the tinkling of bells and often worked themselves into a frenzy of emotion.

These ritual dances and ceremonies helped the Indians gain great physical strength and endurance, and taught them to develop cooperation and group consciousness. The American Indians and the Mongolians of Asia had acquired great physical prowess, and the rituals and ceremonies helped to stimulate them emotionally.

Other religious rituals developed in different parts of the world. Evidences of them are at Stonehenge in England. Explorers have also found relics of ancient rituals on islands in the South Seas. Seers of the Far East believe that a great continent once spread over what is now the South Pacific and Indian Oceans. Australia and many islands are believed to be the highest part of this submerged continent, which is called Lemuria. Speculations are that the first truly human man developed on this continent. The southern part of Asia and the eastern shores of Africa, it is thought, were once part of Lemuria.

In Tanzania, East Africa, Dr. L. S. B. Leakey dug up a skull, which indicates that two million years ago man's earliest ancestors walked upright. If this region was really part of the ancient continent of Lemuria it bears out the idea that the first true human beings developed in that area and there began their early crude religious practices.

On his tour around the world, Captain Cook found relics of some early worshipers on Easter Island. They are statues twenty-seven feet tall, carved of volcanic stone. Some of the unfinished statues are still in the quarries. They represent only the upper part of the body of gigantic men, with unusually long heads and ears. Some of the statues have been taken to the British Museum. Others are in the National Museum in Washington. It is not definitely known if these were objects of worship, or likenesses of ancestors or tribal leaders.

Their great size could mean they were carved by people who were giants themselves. Many myths have been passed down about a race of giants. There is the story in the Bible of Goliath, who was slain by little David with a sling shot. This story may have been told to reveal how a smaller race of people, who had invented weapons for defense, overcame a giant race. The Greeks also told the story of the giant Cyclops who made the thunderbolts that killed Apollo's son.

As the human race developed, men invented tools for tilling the soil, as well as weapons for defense. They stopped wandering about and planted fields, tamed and raised goats and sheep. In the deserts they built shelters of skins, and in the jungles, thatched huts. When they were settled in villages, they also built shelters for their many spirits or gods. The worshipers gathered there to perform their rituals and ceremonies.

Gradually men began to dream of a kind god, who watched over their tribe like a loving father. Eventually each group had its own tribal god, with many lesser gods and spirits under him. One of the tribes that finally settled in western Asia, began to worship only one God, which they called Jehovah. These were

5

the Hebrew people, whose prophets and teachers laid the foundation for three religions: Judaism, Christianity, and Islam.

Much earlier another great religion evolved in India. It developed similar ideas and called the Supreme Creator, Brahman. This religion is known today as Hinduism.

People who had learned the lessons of life more easily than others forged ahead and became the priests and teachers. Many of these tried to learn more about the nature of their God and his will for humanity. Each felt he had made spiritual contact with this great source of life and was inspired to pass on this knowledge to others. Rituals that had earlier been used to appease the anger of the gods, gradually became ceremonies of penance and adoration.

At first there were no written languages. These teachings were given by the priests and memorized by the people. But memories were fallible and often the original teachings became distorted before they were finally written down.

When a few advanced people learned to write and read, the teachings that had been passed from teacher to teacher were written down. Most of the tribes explained how the world began. Another favorite story was about a great flood that engulfed the world. Each group described this as if his tribe were the only one to survive the disaster. Everyone is familiar with the story in the Bible of how Noah saved his family and two of each animal species in the ark.

The Cherokee Indians of North America have their version also of this great catastrophe. According to the legends told around their evening camp fires, there was once a dog who went down to the river every day and howled. When his master scolded him, the dog said, "Very soon there is going to be a great freshet (flood). The water will come so high everybody will be drowned. But if you will build a raft to hold your family you will be saved."

The man argued with the dog, but finally believed what he said. He built a raft and put plenty of food on it. When the rains started, he took his family aboard and they were saved. It rained for a very long time until even the mountains were covered and all the rest of the people were drowned.

The rains finally stopped and the water went down, so the man took his family ashore. When he looked on the other side of the mountain, he saw the bones of all the drowned people.

In another of the Cherokee myths there was an eagle on the raft. When the rain stopped the man sent him out to look for dry land so the raft could land. The eagle flew over the wet earth. According to the myth every time he lowered his wings a valley was pushed down, and every time he raised them a mountain was pulled up, so the Cherokee country has been mountainous ever since.

Explorers of the ocean bottom have been making discoveries that may someday give evidence that the flood stories passed down in various religious scriptures were based on real history. Some of the great seers and teachers claim that a large continent once existed where the Atlantic now rolls. This was gradually sunk by a series of earthquakes and floods that affected much of the world. The Bahamas, the Antilles, and other Atlantic islands could have been peaks of this great continent, Atlantis. The Greek philosopher, Plato, wrote about this sunken continent.

According to the legends, a high type of civilization developed there. However when some of the people began to use their newly-acquired powers for selfish ends, trouble fell upon them. The more spiritually developed people were warned of pending disaster and migrated to east and west to settle on land that later became the Americas, Europe, and North Africa. After this the great continent was gradually destroyed by earthquakes and tidal waves.

Today we find in the Americas, Europe, Egypt, and Asia various versions of this flood story. Other evidences point to the theory that these scattered peoples stemmed from the same source. In the temples and pyramids of Peru, Mexico, and Egypt may be found symbolic carvings that seem to indicate that these widely scattered groups may have a common background of religious culture.

As the ages passed, religious ideas and rituals changed. Thousands of years before Christ one group of Aryans settled in India. Their seers were inspired to teach the people hymns about the creation and the Creator, and to establish rules for right living. These early teachings are contained in what is now known as the Vedas, which means knowledge. At first these were taught orally and passed down from generation to generation before anyone knew how to read and write. Some researchers date them back to 6000 B.C. About 1500 B.C., more than a thousand of these were finally put into writing. They are now known as the *Rig-Veda*, probably the oldest scriptures in the world. The religion taught in the Vedas is still followed today, in modified form, by about 300 million people in India and 150 million in other parts of the world. It is known as Hinduism.

Suggested Further Reading:

ATKINS, G. G. and BRADEN, C. S.
  Procession of the Gods, Harper & Bros., New York, 1939.

BHAGAVAN DAS
  The Essential Unity of All Religions, The Theosophical Publishing House, Wheaton, Illinois, 1966 (Quest Book paperback).

EUNSTADTER, PETER
  Living With Thailand's Gentle Lua, The National Geographic, Washington, D. C., July 1966.

FRAZER, JAMES GEORGE
  The Golden Bough, 8 vols., St. Martin's Press, New York, 1963.

GAER, JOSEPH
  How the Great Religions Began, Apollo Editions, Inc., New York, 1968 (paperback).

POWELL, J. W.
  Nineteenth Annual Report of the Bureau of American Ethnology, Government Printing Office, Washington, D. C., 1900.

SEATS, LAVALL
  Africa, Arrows to Atoms, Convention Press, Nashville, Tenn., 1967.

SPARKS, JOHN B.
  The Histomap of Religion, Chart, Rand McNally, Chicago, 1966.

SQUIRES, JOHN L. and McLEAN, R. E.
  American Indian Dances, The Ronald Press, New York, 1963.

TOYNBEE, ARNOLD
  An Historian's Approach to Religion, Oxford University Press, New York, 1956.

Meenakshi Hindu Temple at Madurai in South India.

Photograph by A. Devaney, Inc., N. Y.

Chapter II

The Path of Hinduism

The One and the Many

The Hindus believe that beyond all manifestation there is the Absolute, the All, the *Para-brahman*. This Absolute is without any attribute, as it is indivisible, is above all qualities and is boundless. It is also believed that in the region of the manifest there is a Supreme Being at the head of a Hierarchy of Divine Beings. Many others beside the Hindus recognize this as basic truth. Brahman, the Supreme Being, is like a diamond with many facets. We must always keep in mind that the Hindu names given to the Deity and its various forms of manifestation apply to the same eternal verities that other religious groups call by different names.

Hinduism has the concept of Brahman (God) manifesting as a Trinity: Brahma the Creator, Vishnu the Preserver, and Shiva the Destroyer. This belief is similar to the Christian idea of Father, Son, and Holy Ghost; body, soul, and spirit in the individual. In addition to these, the triune aspects of the One, who have their special work of presiding over the various departments of human

11

and world development, there is a host of invisible helpers called *devas*. In Christianity, Judaism, and Islam they are called angels and archangels. Most of the religions also recognize that these angelic hosts have many lesser helpers, also invisible to the physical eye, as the fine substance of their bodies does not register on the average retina. These have been called fairies, elves, pixies, and brownies. However, in different countries they are called by various other names. The folklore of every race has fascinating tales of how these elfish beings help the work of the *devas* or angels. Though these tales may seem fanciful they convey inner truths, just as the parables of Jesus were told to dramatize many lessons.

The Hindu Trinity

Each of the three manifestations of Brahman — Brahma, Vishnu, and Shiva — has its special work to do in the world. Brahma creates the substances out of which the world is built for minerals, plants, animals, and man. Vishnu, the Preserver, guides the development of this life or consciouness, especially in man. From time to time the spirit of Vishnu comes down to earth and is born in a physical body to teach people the laws of life and the ways to purify themselves. This happens at intervals when humanity has broken so many laws it is desperately in need of help.

Shiva destroys old forms to prepare for new ones. Thus continents are changed by earthquakes and tidal waves to make way for new land. Worn-out physical bodies distintegrate to free souls for more lessons in other lives. The work of Shiva is necessary, for old ideas no longer useful for man's development must give way to new. The child in the third grade no longer needs the guidelines he used for writing in the first. So useless rituals and forms must be replaced by those a more developed soul can understand.

All about us we see constant change. In the fall the sap flows downward, leaves die and fall. The tree rests and comes forth in greater glory in the spring. The caterpillar weaves a cocoon for a long rest, then the cocoon is destroyed to release a brilliantly-colored butterfly. Man's body is destroyed at death to free the soul for a period of rest and an eventual return in a new and better body.

Change is necessary if humanity is to reach its goal of perfection. All about us are evidences that even the physical earth is in a process of constant change. Storms and earthquakes destroy old lands, while new islands rise out of the seas. Shells have been found buried on mountain sides, proving they were once under water. All this the Hindus believe is the work of the third aspect of the Trinity, Shiva.

Most Hindus give their adoration to either Vishnu or Shiva. There are many lesser gods, who preside over various departments of people's lives, so that Hinduism is a religion of many gods, helping the over-all Brahman. Shrines, temples, and statues have been built to these. Almost every Hindu household has its special god, or protective helper, and a shrine where prayers and offerings are made.

Along the highways simple folk are often seen praying, or placing coconuts, fruit, or gifts of flowers at some small shrine. There are shops near the temples where offerings may be bought to place in the lamp-lit inner shrine. If a person is beginning a journey, or seeking a job, he offers gifts and asks help of Ganesha, one who removes obstacles, or the god of success. A youth on his way to school to take a test will offer flowers or coconuts or just a prayer at the shrine of Ganesha.

World Teachers

In the Great Plan for humanity teachers have been sent to various races and religious groups in times of great need. There have been several of these teachers in India. The last three were Rama, Krishna, and Gautama Buddha. The Hindus believe that Vishnu, the second aspect of their Trinity, taught through these teachers and will take another body to help humanity climb toward perfection. In the same way the Christians believe the Christ will come again to help the world. Many believe the Christ spirit used the Master Jesus' body in Palestine two thousand years ago.

In the Hindu scripture, the *Bhagavad-Gita,* Krishna said:

For the protection of the good, for the destruction of evil-doers, for firmly establishing dharma (law) I am born from age to age.

13

This second aspect of the Trinity, called Vishnu in Hinduism, the Son or Christ in Christianity, also inspired other teachers. This divine spirit guided Abraham, Isaiah, Moses, and other prophets to teach the Hebrews in western Asia. It also incarnated in Palestine as Jesus, who became the Christ and whose teachings are now followed by millions all over the world. With similar inspiration, Confucius taught his philosophy in China. The same spirit inspired Mohammed in Arabia to help people there to win millions of Muslims to follow his teachings. So this second aspect of the Trinity, by whatever name it may be called, has brought spiritual teachings to many lands and races.

This idea of a divine Hierarchy is easier to understand as we see priests, rabbis, and ministers needing a staff of assistants to help with their work. So it is believed that every aspect of world progress is directed by advanced beings in the spiritual Hierarchy. Government, science, the arts, religion, social welfare, all have advanced souls guiding the inner phases of development in these areas. Even the least of us may help along our particular line and feel the direction of those Great Ones, who are trying to make a better world.

Reincarnation and Karma

Reincarnation and karma are essential concepts of the Hindu teachings. Reincarnation means simply that a man is a soul and must be born again and again in many bodies before he can attain the perfection of a god-like man. Through life after life, in both male and female bodies, in different castes and races, the soul learns the laws of life until selfish desires are mastered and he becomes one with his spiritual self. In the *Bhagavad-Gita,* an important Hindu scripture, rebirth is explained:

> As a man, casting off worn-out garments, taketh new ones, so the dweller in the body, casting off worn-out bodies, entereth into others that are new.

The kind of body the soul will enter in the next incarnation is conditioned by the kind of life the man led in his earlier lives.

Science teaches that for every action there is a reaction. Karma may be described in that way, as the law of cause and effect. The Hindu *Mahabharata,* a great epic poem, of which the *Bhagavad-Gita* is a part, describes karma:

Like fishes going against a current of water, the acts of a past life are flung back on the actor. The embodied creature experiences happiness for his good acts and misery for his evil ones.

St. Paul explained the same divine law in the Christian Bible centuries later when he said:

Be not deceived; God is not mocked: whatsoever a man soweth that shall he also reap.

So the Hindu accepts his place in life with quiet resignation. He knows the divine laws are just. If he has broken them he must suffer the consequences. If he is born in good circumstances, in wealth and comfort and with many opportunities, he believes he has earned that station by good conduct in earlier lives. Those not so fortunate are inspired to better living in hopes of higher stations in their future incarnations.

Caste

When the Aryans came to India they were divided into four sections, according to their tasks in daily life, but were all part of one group. The Brahmins, highly educated, were the teachers and priestly class. The Kshattriyas were rulers and warriors. The Vaishyas or merchant class attended to buying and selling. The Sudras did the labor, such as tilling the soil, milking cows, cooking, and cleaning. As time went by, these four sections crystallized into caste.

The Hindus believed if a man lived a good life, no matter what his caste, he could be born again in a Brahmin body. Since India gained her independence from Britain the rigid caste system is no longer prevalent and has begun to change. There are now marriages between castes. Such social reformers as Mahatma Gandhi have done much to improve conditions of the people, so that many previously considered as the "untouchables" are now highly educated and occupy important positions of state.

Sacred Literature

The *Rig-Veda* of Hinduism is thought to be the oldest religious scripture in the world. In addition there are three other collections of Vedas: the *Yajur-Veda*, the *Atharva-Veda*, and the *Sama-Veda*. The *Atharva-Veda*, besides other philosophical topics, deals with magic, good and evil, while the *Sama-Veda* through its chants reveals the science of music. The *Yajur-Veda* is like the *Rig-Veda* and contains selected verses from the *Rig-Veda* with many original prose formulas and chants.

The Upanishads are many in number. There are 108 of the more important. Of these, twelve are called major, and the others minor. These teach the way of wisdom that leads to a realization of Brahman or the divinity within each man. They represent the earliest form of Hindu religion. Even today it is a common sight in the villages in India to see groups of people sitting under trees, discussing with their guru the meaning of the Vedas.

As the centuries passed, the teachings and rituals changed. In ancient times the country was divided into small kingdoms, ruled by fabulously wealthy kings. Many heroic tales of these ancient rulers were told by wandering story tellers; most of the tales were filled with religious significance and symbolism. Some of the greatest of these were written down in the *Mahabharata* which has 90,000 stanzas and is one of the longest poems in all literature. It is said to have been composed by a sage called Vyasa. Another great epic is the *Ramayana,* given by the sage Valmiki.

The Story of Rama

In the *Ramayana* symbols and folklore are used to teach people how to destroy evil. When lawlessness and evil held sway in India, the second aspect of the Hindu Trinity, Vishnu, decided to take a physical body to help the people, so he was born in the body of Rama, son to Dasaratha, King of Ayodhya in northern India. In his youth Rama and his brother Lakshmana were taken by their teacher to the court of Janaka, the ruler of the neighboring kingdom of Videha. There Rama won the hand of Sita, the beautiful daughter of Janaka, by lifting and wielding the bow of Shiva.

After their marriage the happy couple lived in the royal palace in Ayodhya. When Dasaratha grew old he wanted Rama to become king. However his second and favorite wife, Kaikeyi, on the coronation day said he had promised her two wishes, and she wanted as one of the wishes that Bharata, her son, inherit the throne. The other wish was that Rama should leave the country and live in a forest for fourteen years. Rama felt, on hearing this, that his father should keep his promise. So with his wife, Sita, and his brother, Lakshmana, Rama went into exile, though Sita had to plead with him to take her along. When he finally consented she willingly gave up all her fine clothes and jewels to follow him into the forest where they lived as hermits.

The king died, broken hearted. Bharata refused to be crowned king and took only interim charge of the kingdom. In the forest Rama, Sita, and Lakshmana helped the nearby villagers to kill many demons who had annoyed the sages living in the hermitages. Once while Rama and his brother were out trying to capture alive a golden deer (a demon in disguise) which Sita had seen and wanted to have as her pet, the king of the demons, Ravana, stole Sita and took her in an aerial car to his palace in Lanka (Ceylon).

Rama asked Hanuman, the king of the monkeys, to help rescue his wife. Hanuman in his search was led to Ravana's court, where he found Sita. A great army of monkeys and bears was organized. They built a causeway across the sea of Lanka. During the fierce battle that ensued, Ravana and the demons were destroyed and Sita rescued.

Sita reported she had been treated with respect in Ravana's palace, but she had rejected his proposal to marry him. However, since she had lived in the home of another man, Rama could not take her back unless she was proven pure, in front of all. In great grief Sita threw herself into a fire, invoking the fire god that if she were innocent he would help her to prove it. So the fire god, Agni, did not burn her, but brought her resplendent and pure to Rama. This miracle proved her innocence, so Rama and Sita with Lakshmana returned to their kingdom as the fourteen years had come to an end. Bharata rejoiced at their return and handed over the throne to Rama, who on an auspicious day was crowned king.

This account is also one of the many episodes and hero stories of the *Mahabharata*. Vishnu had incarnated in Rama to destroy the evil demons, which were personified by their king, Ravana. Sita, Rama's wife, is still regarded with special reverence by Hindu women, for she was the ideal wife, devoted and faithful to her husband. The Hindus repeat this and other stories over and over for their character building value, just as Christians tell the stories of the Prodigal Son or the parable of the talents. The Hindu stories are often set to music and sung in the temples and at music festivals.

17

The Bhagavad-Gita

A chapter in the epic poem *Mahabharata* is the *Bhagavad-Gita*. This is a long, inspiring story which is one of India's scriptures. It has been translated into many languages, because it helps students of all religions to develop courage and devotion. Krishna, the hero of the story, is regarded as the later incarnation of Vishnu. He is a charioteer in the story, speaking with supreme wisdom of Vishnu, the teacher. He explains to Arjuna the meaning of his experiences. A stanza from the poem explains the purpose of Krishna's coming:

> Whenever the sacred law fails, and evil raises its head I take
> embodied birth,
> To guard the righteous and root out the sinners and establish
> the sacred law.
> I am born from age to age.

Krishna, embodiment of divine love, is worshiped with great warmth by millions in India, just as Jesus is adored by Christians and Mohammed by the Muslims.

Krishna incarnated long before Jesus of Nazareth, yet the stories of their childhoods are quite similar. In the *Bhagavatam* — one of the Puranas or ancient legends that deal among other things with the origin of the universe and man and the history of remote times — it is narrated that when King Kamsa, an uncle of Krishna, heard that his sister's eighth son would kill him and take the kingdom, he ordered all boys of that family slain. So Krishna and his older brother were hidden in the house of a cowherd. In a similar way when King Herod heard rumors that the Holy Child Jesus would grow up and rule a great kingdom, he ordered all baby boys under two years old to be killed. Then Joseph and Mary fled with their son to Egypt. Both Jesus and Krishna performed many miracles through the power of their indwelling divinity.

In the *Bhagavad-Gita,* Arjuna, one of the heroes, prepares to go into battle against his cousins and his elders, teachers and former friends who are arrayed on the opposite side. As he waits in his chariot to begin the battle he becomes sick at heart at the thought of fighting those who are all still dear to him. Krishna, his charioteer, explains that Arjuna can only slay their bodies, not

18

their souls:

> As a man puts off his worn out clothes
> and puts on other new ones
> So the embodied spirit puts off worn out bodies
> and goes to others that are new.

Krishna includes many of the inspiring teachings of the Hindu religion. He says that men must learn to do their duty without desiring rewards. In one of the verses he explains, "There is more joy in doing one's own duty badly, than in doing another's duty well."

The *Bhagavad-Gita* teaches many truths that help all people of whatever religion, for they are based on eternal laws. It has much profound meaning, and actually it is believed that the war described on the battlefield symbolizes in each of us the struggle against evil, and each warrior is a symbol of an unwanted characteristic that must be conquered.

Images

Hindus regard their images, shrines, and temples with great reverence. The more advanced in wisdom realize that the images are only symbols of the Supreme Being, but the majority of the people need some physical image to keep them reminded of spiritual things. Superstitions have developed because many people have not been able to understand the true meaning behind the symbols. Our own Protestant and Catholic churches are filled with beautiful art in stained glass windows and statues that help to tune people in to the spiritual, so we should be understanding of others who cling to those images which give them hope of refuge in a power beyond themselves.

Temples

India is a land of many temples. They form a center of the community and have a great influence on the lives of the people. Much of the wealth of the temples is used for education and charity. In the middle ages temples were great centers of learning and of art. They were also used as places of refuge for the sick, homeless, and aged. Even now in many temples a large number of the poorer classes are given free food, after the worship is over.

There are about 1500 temples in Benares, now called Varanasi, the most holy city of India, though all the temples are not Hindu. Every Hindu longs to make a pilgrimage to Varanasi once in his life. He believes if he bathes in the sacred waters of the river Ganga (Ganges), supposed to have descended from heaven, he will be cured of any sickness and that the waters will cleanse all evil from his life.

Scenes along the banks of the Ganga, near one of the temples, are colorful and full of activity: some people bathe while others wash clothes. Families bring their dead to the river bank to burn their bodies on funeral pyres, and to sprinkle their ashes in the sacred river. Many Hindus believe this custom frees the soul from all sins, so that it goes straight to the heaven world. The eldest son must perform this rite for his father.

Along the roadsides all over India are small shrines, where Hindus may stop and worship. Every village has a shrine or small temple. In the earlier days temples were very simple shrines, many being dug out of the hills or mountain sides. Most of these were unadorned shelters, containing a shrine for the deity. Later the solid rocks were polished and columns and ornaments added. There are many fine cave temples in India, such as the Elephanta and Ellora caves. Their vaulted, arched ceilings have been chiseled out of solid rock. The walls have ornamental columns with carved figures.

The era of cave temples faded as more elaborate temples with beautiful sculptures were built in the villages and cities. The most ornate of these is the temple at Madurai. Its high towers on four sides are covered with life-size plaster figures, depicting the stories of Hindu gods and goddesses. This temple was finally completed in 1660, but by the twentieth century its main tower needed repairs. The Hindus, assisted by UNESCO, spent $378,000 to have it restored.

This temple has some very exquisite sculpture carved in granite in the courtyard. In south India there are many big temples like this that are famous for their beautiful art and sculpture.

There is no congregational worship in Hindu temples, such as in Christian churches. People go alone or in family groups to sit quietly and meditate on the sacred scriptures. Priests are available in the temples to perform *puja* (worship) for individuals or groups. In the larger temples there are halls or open spaces where people gather to listen to the reading or dramatization of epic

Pilgrims bathing in the Ganga (Ganges) River at Varanasi (Benares) in northern India. Two Hindu temples are in the background.

Hindu literature, or classic music with a religious theme. Some of the temples also have within their courtyards rest homes for pilgrims.

Ceremonies and Festivals

According to the ancient customs observed by the Hindus there was always great rejoicing in the home when a son was born. The mother had long prayed she would have a son to carry on his father's name. Immediately after birth a sacred mantra (prayer) was whispered in his ear, and his lips were touched with a mixture of honey and ghee (butter).

The father, especially, was happy. For the Hindus believed there was no glory in heaven for a man who had no son. It was also necessary to perform the funeral rites for his father, to insure his safe crossing to the other world.

The following are some of the ceremonies and customs which used to be observed by certain groups. Contacts with the western world have changed many of those practices in recent times. However many of the old rites, in simplified form, are still observed by many families.

Among some groups in ancient times, soon after the birth of a baby, members of the family went out blowing horns and ringing bells to announce the good news. The family astrologer would cast the baby's horoscope. If the child was a boy he was named after one of the many Hindu gods; if a girl, she was given the name of a goddess. Ten days later, at a ceremony corresponding to western christening, the naming ritual was held when the father whispered the child's name into his ear. The mother stood on a prayer rug and asked Savitr, the Sun-God, to bless him. There was another ceremony when the child was given its first solid food at the age of six months. This was generally rice mixed with ghee.

In the old days there was not as much joy over the birth of a girl, although she was also loved and petted as she grew up. But times have changed. Now there is as much joy over the birth of a girl as of a boy, and equal opportunities and equal shares of wealth are given to both. Childhood among the more prosperous in India is a very happy time. Tamed animals, especially cows, which are considered sacred, because of their representing in symbol the Cosmic Cow, the mother of infinite creation, form part of the household. Beautiful gardens have small shrines among the flowers where children make offerings and prayers. At almost every street corner is a small shrine where people worship every day.

In the old days a boy's life followed a very rigid pattern. If he belonged to the Brahmin class, the highest and priestly class, he had the "Sacred Thread Ceremony" at the age of seven. This is similar to "Confirmation" in the Christian Church. For this ritual the boy was dressed like a holy man and carried a staff. The officiating priest placed a thread loop made of three strands of cotton over his left shoulder and under his right arm. As he did so the father whispered into the boy's ear the holy mantra (prayer) from the *Rig-Veda* called the Gayatri: "Let us think on the holy splendor of the god Savitr, that he may inspire our minds."

The three strands in the thread reminded him of control of thought, action, and desire. This ritual marked the end of childhood and the beginning of the student's learning period. Three times a day, at sunrise, noon, and sunset, he repeated the Gayatri. In addition there were other prayers, chants, and rhythmic breathing, postures and gestures. Gurus (teachers) gave the boy instructions in these practices.

The outer form of investing the boy with the sacred thread is followed even now, but in a simpler fashion.

In the past until he was seven a Brahmin boy was instructed at home by a guru, then he was sent to an *ashrama* or forest hermitage to study the Vedas, Upanishads, and other scriptures. Sitting cross-legged on the ground, young Hindus listened while their gurus explained the sacred writings. They learned the basic principles of Hindu religion and philosophy — the triune aspect of the One God, the law of cause and effect or karma, the path of evolution by reincarnation, and the manifestation of the One Principle in all beings and things.

One of the important Hindu celebrations is the Festival of Lights called *Dipavali* (sometimes spelled *Diwali*). This is similar to our New Year. At this fall festival in North India every home and public building is decorated with small oil lamps or candles. The heads of families close all old accounts and receive the blessings of the priests on their well-kept records. Houses are often re-painted, new clothing bought, visits made to relatives and friends, and a better life planned for the future. If a girl lives near a river she may put a candle on a tiny raft and set it adrift downstream. If the candle burns as long as she can see it floating away she will have good fortune in the coming year.

In the South it is a festival symbolic of the destruction of evil and triumph of the good. People take holy baths, wear new clothes, decorate their houses with coconut and mango leaves, draw designs on the floor with rice flour, and have great feasts. Fireworks form an important feature of the celebration.

The Holi festival, observed in most parts of India, except in the south, comes in spring and is somewhat similar to Hallowe'en. It is based on the legend of a witch who was burned. Young people gather brush to make a bonfire. All join in the fun of marching around the fire and singing joyously about the slain witch. Boys buy red dye at the street vendor's to dissolve in water and spray on the merrymakers.

Another fall festival called *Dasara* in the south, and *Durga Puja* in the north, honors the Mother Goddess. By worshipers of Shiva, she is called by several names, Gauri the Virtuous, and Durga, the Inaccessible One. She is also worshiped by followers of Vishnu as Lakshmi. Images picture her slaying a demon to show that evil must be destroyed. In her gentle nature she is worshiped as the compassionate mother. Other statues of her show her with her husband, Shiva. According to the legends, in one of her incarnations, when her father quarreled with her husband, she threw herself on a funeral pyre. Her ashes were blown over the country and wherever they fell, shrines have been built to her. On her festival day flowers and fruit are placed at her shrines, and there is dancing and purification by fire.

In January the harvest festival of *Samkaranthi* is celebrated all over India, when the sun is worshiped and a sweet rice dish called "pongal," made of freshly harvested rice, is offered, along with newly cut sugarcane. This is generally a three day festival when the last day is observed as animals' day, on which occasion the animals are gaily decorated and taken out in processions.

The Hindu festival, *Janmashtami,* is similar to the Christian Christmas. This August festival is for the most beloved teacher, Krishna. The evening before, or even several days in advance, worshipers meet in the temples to hear the story of the infant Krishna, who had to be hidden from a jealous king and brought up by a cowherd. The image of the little Krishna is bathed and dressed, placed in a cradle and worshiped. Next morning the image is taken to the nearby river, and the people go in boats out into the water to drop the image in mid-stream, where it will be safe. If there is no river nearby the image is dropped in a small man-made lake.

One of the most elaborate and expensive Hindu ceremonies is that of marriage. In the old days child marriages were frequent, but now the laws of India forbid a girl under 14 to marry. In most cases her parents consult with the future husband's father and mother. An astrologer compares the couple's horoscopes to see if they are suited to each other and chooses the date for the wedding.

The ritual of the ceremony is based on instructions in the *Rig-Veda,* the oldest of Hindu scriptures. Often the family of the bride goes into debt to provide her with fine clothes, a dowry, and a feast. In North India the bride puts away her white sari which she has worn as a child, and is dressed in fine clothes with a sheer veil over her dark, long hair. Before going out to meet her future husband for the first time, she stops at a shrine to Ganesha, the god of success, to pray for a happy marriage.

The bridegroom, dressed in his finest, goes with his family and friends to the home of the bride. He is received by the bride's parents with a ceremonial drink of honey and curds. The ceremony is performed under a large canopy before a sacred fire. A curtain under the canopy separates the two sides from which the bride and groom enter. When the curtain is drawn before the ceremony the bride and groom see each other for the first time. After the father gives the bride away, the hours-long ritual continues with the chanting of many verses from the Vedas. As part of the ceremony, rice and ghee are poured on the sacred fire to the chanting of mantras. The groom then ties the marriage emblem around the bride's neck, and takes the bride's hand, promising to be true to her. He holds it while she sprinkles rice on the fire. Their garments are knotted together, and holding their right hands they walk around the fire. After this she steps on a millstone while he steps on grains of rice in the path as they take seven steps to-gether. They are then sprinkled with holy water. After the feast, dancing and music, she is taken to the home of her husband, where she will live the rest of her life.

Marriage in the south is somewhat different. The bride is not veiled, nor is there a curtain separating the bride and groom. Some of these early customs are outdated and now the families sit and eat together, though in the old days the wife never ate with her husband.

Formerly a woman left a widow could not marry again. Her life was one of great misery, and during the middle ages when Sati was prevalent among the Hindus, many widows threw themselves on their husband's funeral pyre rather than live alone. In recent times, however, Hindu widows' lives are much improved. They may remarry or go to schools where they are trained to be nurses or teachers, or enter other businesses. Many Indian girls now choose their own partners, and can secure divorces under certain circumstances.

So the Hindu religion has gone through many phases, with rituals and customs often changing. The forms of religions have changed with the ages, but the basic laws of life laid down in the Vedas and other scriptures remain eternally the same. It has been in many ways flexible and has absorbed other teachings. It remains still the most ancient of the living religions and has formed the basis out of which many religions and cults have developed.

Suggested Further Reading:

Bhagavad-Gita (Several Editions).

ARNOLD, EDWIN
   The Song Celestial, The Theosophical Publishing House, Wheaton, Illinois, 1970 (Quest Book paperback).

BASHAM, A. L.
   The Wonder That Was India, Sidgwick & Jackson, London, 1954.

BESANT, ANNIE
   Seven Great Religions—Hinduism, The Theosophical Publishing House, Adyar, Madras, India, 1966.

DE BARY, WM. THEODORE
   Sources of Indian Tradition, vol. 1, Columbia University Press, New York, 1967.

FRAZIER, ALLIE M.
   Readings in Eastern Religious Thought: Hinduism, The Westminster Press, Philadelphia, 1969.

HIRIYANNA, M.
   Essentials of Indian Philosophy, George Allen & Unwin, London, 1961.

MORGAN, KENNETH
   Religion of the Hindus, The, Donald Press Co., New York, 1953.

PRABHAVANANDA, SWAMI and
ISHERWOOD, CHRISTOPHER (trans.)
   The Song of God, Bhagavad-Gita. Introduction by Aldous Huxley, Harper & Bros., New York, 1951.

RADHAKRISHNAN, SARVEPALLI
   Hindu View of Life, George Allen & Unwin, London, 1961.

RADHAKRISHNAN, S, and MOORE, CHARLES A.
   A Source Book in Indian Philosophy, Princeton University, Princeton, New Jersey, 1957.

RAGHAVAN, V.
   The Indian Heritage, The Indian Institute of World Culture, Bangalore, India, 1963.

RAJAGOPALACHARI, C.
   Hinduism: Doctrine and Way of Life. Bharatiya Vidya Bhavan, Bombay, India, 1964 (Bhavan's Book University Series).

RENOU, LOUIS
   Hinduism, George Braziller, New York, 1962. Washington Square Press, 1963 (paperback).

SANATANA-DHARMA
   Elementary and *Advanced Textbook of Hindu Religion and Ethics,* The Theosophical Publishing House, Adyar, Madras, India, 1966.

27

SCOFIELD, JOHN
   India, National Geographic, Washington, D. C., May, 1963.

SHARMA, CHANDRAHAR
   A Critical Survey of Indian Philosophy, Motilal Banarsidass, Delhi,
   India, 1964.

SILVERSTONE, MERILYN
   Royal Wedding in Jaisalmer, National Geographic, Washington, D. C.,
   January, 1965.

Chapter III

The Path of Buddhism

Siddhartha Gautama Buddha

About 600 B.C. the Hindu religion became very dogmatic and set in its outlook, as has been the case with other religions long after the original teachings were given. Hinduism had become more a religion of rituals and ceremonies, and the priestly class held sway over the majority of the simple people. The caste system became very rigid. The profound philosophy and religious truths gave way to blind beliefs and superstitions of the majority. As Krishna had said in the *Bhagavad-Gita*: "Whenever the sacred law fails, and evil raises its head, I take embodied form."

So a new teacher was born in Northern India, Siddhartha Gautama, who became the Buddha. His followers now number many millions all over the world. Gautama's father was King Suddhodhama, ruler of Sakyas, an Aryan tribe living in the foothills of the Himalayas, according to tradition. His mother, Maya Devi, had a dream which a Brahman astrologer interpreted to mean that she would bear a son, who would be either a great emperor or a universal teacher.

Maya Devi wanted her son to be born in the home of her parents, as was the custom. She started on her journey, but did not reach her destination in time. Her son was born on the night of the full moon in May 625 B.C., in Lumbini Gardens. Archaeologists identified the spot two centuries later during the reign of King Asoka. The site was marked by a stupa, or memorial mound. One tradition says the remarkable child took seven steps soon after he was born and said, "This is my last birth. Henceforth there is no more birth for me."

The king wanted his son to inherit the kingdom, but he feared the astrologer's prediction that Siddhartha might become a wandering teacher, so he did everything in his power to prevent it. The boy was kept within the high-walled palace grounds. He was shielded from knowing anything about poverty and suffering. Every luxury was lavished upon him.

The boy showed, even while very young, that he already knew what his *gurus* tried to teach him. As he was of the Kshattriya class, he was trained in military skills, archery, chariot riding and all the sports of the day. Early he exhibited the qualities of love and compassion of a Buddha. The story is told of how he rescued a wounded bird, whose wing had been pierced by an arrow. When the hunter came to claim his game, Siddhartha had revived it and refused to give it up, saying that he who had given it back its life had more right to it than one who had tried to kill it. When an elder was consulted he agreed that Siddhartha was right.

When the time came for him to marry, Siddhartha competed in a tournment with other youths for the choice of a maiden. The girls' fathers had brought them to witness the tournament. When Siddhartha won, he chose his cousin, Yashodara, for his bride. They were married when he was sixteen. The king built them three beautiful palaces, one each for the hot, cold, and rainy seasons. These were surrounded by walled gardens filled with flowers, singing birds, and colorful peacocks. In these palaces Siddhartha and his wife lived an idyllic life. Eventually they had a son, Rahula. Before the boy was born, however, Gautama began to be discontented with his life of luxury and pleasure. He wanted to know what was beyond the palace walls. So the King tried to make sure he would see nothing unpleasant and arranged for his charioteer, Channa, to go around the city which was decorated and beautified for the young prince's visit. But while they rode, an old grey-haired man with tottering legs appeared. The sight shocked Gautama. Later he passed a beggar, faint with hunger. When the chariot drove past a funeral procession with a bereaved family, Gautama's heart was torn with sympathy. "Why is there such suffering, poverty, and misery?" he asked himself. After that Gautama yearned to go out into the world until he found the cause of sorrow and suffering.

As time passed, the call to go out into the world became more insistent. On the full-moon night in May he finally decided to leave his wife and young son and search until he found the meaning of the world's troubles. He was then twenty-nine years old. He asked Channa to saddle his horse, Kanthaka, while the inmates of the palace were sleeping. He and his servant then slipped quietly through the palace gate, for the guard had also been thrown into deep sleep.

Beyond his father's kingdom, near the river Anoma, Gautama dismounted, stripped off his jewels and fine clothes, and put on the yellow robe of a wandering monk. He cut his long hair with his sword, and sent it back to his father by Channa, along with his jewels and clothes. His horse dropped dead of grief when Gautama started off with only a begging bowl and staff, to live the life of an ascetic.

He had heard of five sages, who lived in the forest near Uruvala, so he went there, and listened to their teachings. They were emaciated after long years of denying themselves any comforts or sufficient food. They believed that by these austerities they might gain freedom from the round of rebirths. Gautama became their leader, but soon realized he would not find the answer to suffering by these practices, so he left them.

A Hindu holy man, Kalama Alara, taught him how to meditate, which meant stilling the physical body, the emotions and the mind, so the spiritual self could help in his search for truth. For six years he stayed alone in the forests, meditating. Occasionally he went out with his begging bowl to ask for a few grains of rice or sesame seed to keep his body alive. Finally he became so weak and emaciated he fell to the ground unconscious. When he was found, he was thought to be dead. He finally roused himself and

31

realized that enlightenment could never come by such austerities.

Near the river Neranjara he sat down under a banyan tree. A nobleman's daughter, Sujata, passed and saw he was near starvation. She brought him a bowl of rice and milk. Gautama bathed first in the river, then ate the food. Feeling better, he went into the nearby forest to meditate on what course to take. He decided he must eat in order to have strength to become wise.

Under a bodhi tree at Gaya he sat facing east to continue his search for enlightenment. At first the Devas (angels) surrounded him, pouring their loving power upon him. Then Mara, the spirit of evil, to test him, came in disguise as a messenger to report that his wife had been carried away and his father thrown into prison. But Gautama did not heed these lures back to the old life of luxury. A kingdom was offered him, but he could not be enticed by worldly things.

In spite of the temptations, Gautama continued his meditation. He was not praying to any of the traditional Hindu gods, but trying to become aware of the divine spark within him, to make it glow more brightly through linking it with the infinite source of light. He was like someone in a dark room, trying to plug in a light to make contact with the source of electric power.

Finally Gautama caught visions of his past lives, and understood why he had to have many births. He had had to come back life after life to make adjustments for laws broken in previous lives, and to learn new lessons for advancement in the school of life. He now understood that all suffering was the effect of breaking the laws of physical, emotional, mental, and spiritual life. He believed that the middle way was best, without extremes of indulgence or austerities.

He had been meditating under the bodhi tree for forty-nine days when on the full moon of May, these truths were revealed to him. After that he was called the Enlightened One, or the Buddha. For the word *Buddha* does not mean a person, but a stage of spiritual attainment. He was not born as a Buddha, but became the Buddha by living in harmony with divine laws. In a similar way others may attain Buddhahood, if they follow the Master's teachings.

After his enlightenment, the Buddha returned to the deer park at Saranath near Varanasi to tell his five former companions

Buddhist Temple at Bodh Gaya, marking the place where Gautama attained enlightenment.

what he had learned. This was later written down as remembered by his disciples:

"There are two extremes, brothers, which he who has given up the world must avoid. What are the two extremes? A life given to pleasure, devoted to pleasure and to lusts — this is degrading, sensual, vulgar, ignoble, and profitless. And a life given to mortification — this is painful, ignoble, and profitless. By avoiding these two extremes, brothers, I have gained the knowledge of the Middle Way, which leads to insight, which leads to wisdom, which conduces to calm, to knowledge, and to supreme enlightenment. It is the Noble Eightfold Path."

The Four Noble Truths and The Noble Eightfold Path

Gautama Buddha then explained the Four Noble Truths. The first was that suffering comes in evolutionary growth through birth in life after life. The second explained how sorrow is caused by men's selfish desires. The third urged people to give up their selfish cravings and desires. Last, the Buddha taught how to train oneself to give up these desires and cravings by obeying the spiritual laws and following the Middle Path.

The Buddha then explained more in detail how these high ideals might be attained by following the Noble Eightfold Path: 1. Right Understanding, for without right understanding of the laws of life one can never attain wisdom. 2. Right Thought, which includes the virtues of selflessness and compassion for all. 3. Right Speech, which results from right thought, and excludes falsehood and gossip. 4. Right Action, which excludes all killing, stealing, drinking of intoxicants, and sexual misconduct. 5. Right Livelihood, which excludes selling intoxicants, poisons, human beings, or the slaying of animals. 6. Right Effort, which means trying to prevent the development of evil and the promotion of good already in existence. 7. Right Mindfulness, which is a constant awareness of the physical, emotional, and mental laws of life. 8. Right Concentration or Meditation, which helps develop spiritual growth.

By practicing these great truths the Buddha taught that anyone might attain enlightenment or Nirvana while still in the physical body, as he had done. After hearing his sermons, Ananda, his half brother, was the first to accept the teachings. Others soon followed and became his disciples.

The Teachings Spread

The Buddha traveled up and down the Ganga (Ganges) valley giving many discourses on the Noble Eightfold Path. Soon he had sixty disciples, who spread out over India to carry the teachings to others. So Buddhism became the first missionary movement in religious history. Until that time each country had its own religion, and no effort was made to convert others. The Buddha's message was for all people without distinction of caste or race. Kings, noblemen, and outcasts all became its converts.

On hearing what he was doing King Suddhodana sent for his son, for he was very old and wanted to see him again before he died. On arrival Gautama told his father that he no longer belonged to any one family, but to the whole world for he was now the Buddha, or world teacher. Gautama lived with his family until most of them accepted his teachings. His wife wept on seeing him, for she had missed him very much, and his son, Prince Rahula, asked to inherit his earthly kingdom. His half-brother, Ananda, became one of the most loved of his followers and an authority on his teachings. His wife, his foster-mother, and an aunt were the first to enter an order for female devotees, or *bhikkhunis*.

For forty-five years after attaining enlightenment, the Buddha stayed on in his physical body to help humanity. During the eight dry months of the year, he and his disciples traveled around India teaching all who would listen. The four rainy months were spent in retreats built by wealthy kings who had become converts. Later these retreats became monasteries for the monks. Their time was spent in meditation and memorizing the teachings.

When Gautama Buddha was eighty years old his body was worn out and he knew his work was done. At the time of the full moon in May he entered a grove of trees in Kusinagara, over a hundred miles from Varanasi. He lay down under the trees with his head to the north and gave final instructions to his closest disciples. His last words to them were, "Work out your salvation with diligence." At the moment of the full moon he quietly left his physical body.

After his body was cremated in the usual custom of India,

his ashes were divided among eight kings who had been his followers. Stupas were built in the places where the ashes were deposited.

A New Religion

The Buddha had said he did not want to form a new religion, but rather to reform Hinduism and free the people from formalized rituals and superstitions that had crept into it. However, soon after his death many of the sages and disciples, led by his half-brother Ananda, gathered to try to preserve the teachings. Some could repeat whole sermons. These were memorized and passed down from teacher to teacher for generations, but nothing was written down until later.

During the reign of the great King Asoka the spread of Buddhism was greatly stimulated. Pilgrimages were made to the sacred places, which King Asoka had searched out and marked: Gautama's birthplace, the Tree of Wisdom, the Deer Park at Saranath, and Kusinagara, where he had left his physical body.

By that time Buddhist monks and nuns were living in monasteries, built by the wealthy to gain merit for themselves. It was considered a great honor for a family to have a son or daughter become a Buddhist monk or nun. The Buddha had laid down certain rules for those living in monasteries.

Sometimes young boys only four or five years of age were sent to spend a brief time to learn from monks in the monasteries. This was preceded by a family ritual during which the child was clothed in fine garments and jewels. His head was then shaved, and his clothes changed to a yellow robe. He carried a staff and begging bowl, dramatizing similar events in the Buddha's life. Other boys entered monasteries when about ten or twelve for more advanced instructions. At the end of a certain period a boy could choose to stay on as a student monk or return home to marry and have a family.

While in the monasteries children learned about the Middle Way, and memorized the Four Great Truths and the Noble Eightfold Path. They learned the five great precepts, which all Buddhists, whether monks or laymen, must observe:

I observe the precept to refrain from destroying the life of beings.

I observe the precept to refrain from stealing.
I observe the precept to refrain from unlawful intercourse.
I observe the precept to refrain from false speech.
I observe the precept to refrain from using intoxicants.

The Buddhists put special emphasis on the first, third, and fifth precepts, for breaking these caused the most misery in the world. The child was also taught to meditate.

Sometimes a boy decided to stay on and become a monk. The Buddha had made a law that no one could become a monk or nun without the consent of his father, since his own father had been so grieved at the path he had taken. Girls also went to the nunneries to receive their religious education.

Buddhist Scriptures

Neither the Buddha nor Jesus ever wrote any of his sermons. Those of the Buddha were passed down from disciple to disciple for generations. In the same way Jesus' teachings were repeated by his disciples, and eventually many gospels were written. However, only four of these were selected to be included in the Bible. In the same way the Buddha's sermons were repeated by disciples, who had heard them, and out of these many different sects of Buddhism finally developed.

It was not until 88 B.C., which was 330 years after the passing of Gautama Buddha, that the Buddhist scriptures began to be written down. This work continued for twelve years before they were finished, making a manuscript of over a million and three-quarter words. These are called *Tripitakas,* literally meaning "Three Baskets."

The first part of the *Tripitaka* is the *Vinaya-Pitaka,* or the Basket of Discipline, explaining the rules for the orders of monks and nuns in the monasteries and nunneries. The second is the *Sutta-Pitaka,* or the Basket of Discourses, which contains the sermons and teachings of the Buddha and a few other sermons that had been delivered by his most advanced disciples, such as Ananda. The third is the *Abhidhamma-Pitaka* or the Basket of Ultimate Doctrine. This helps the Buddha's followers reach the coveted goal of enlightenment or Nirvana. The word *nirvana* is generally misunderstood in the West. It does not mean blotting out or extinction as it is often interpreted, but rather the merging of the separated self into the All-Consciousness, where we know as the Christian Bible says, "In Him we live and move and have our being."

Unlike the Christian heaven, which is said to be an after-death state, the Buddhist Nirvana may be attained as the Buddha attained it, while still living in a physical body. The Buddhist enlightenment is similar to the Christian's idea of salvation. By discrimination, desirelessness, good conduct, and love one may attain the goal.

Southern Buddhism

Just as Christianity became divided into Protestant and Catholic sects, so Buddhism had many different interpretations. The two main divisions at first were *Mahayana,* or Northern Buddhism and *Theravada,* or Southern Buddhism. The term *Hinayana* is also used for the Southern School, but as it is objected to by the followers it is not in general use.

Two centuries after the Buddha's passing, Emperor Asoka did more to spread Buddhism than any of the earlier disciples. He sent his son, Mahinda, and his daughter, Sanghamitta, as missionaries to Ceylon. Sanghamitta took with her a branch of the bodhi tree, under which Gautama had attained enlightenment, and planted it at Anuradhapura in 306 B.C. It is said to be one of the oldest trees in the world. Today sixty-four percent of the people of Ceylon are still Buddhists. The teachings there are closer to the original than any other form of Buddhism.

King Asoka secured permission from five Greek kings to send missionaries to Greece. Some also went to Syria and Egypt. It is believed that some of the Buddha's teachings became mingled with those of the Essenes of Palestine. Southern Buddhism, which lays great stress on the Four Noble Truths, the fundamental teachings of the Buddha, also spread to what is now Cambodia, Laos, Vietnam, and Burma.

Temples

The Buddha is said to have given four hairs from his head to a Burmese disciple, who took them back to Burma 2500 years ago. A small stupa was built for this sacred relic. This shrine has been enlarged century after century until today its 326 foot tower

Young students at a school for monks in Burma.

Photograph by A. Devaney, Inc., N. Y.

rises like a shining beacon above the city of Rangoon. In 1871 King Mondon covered the bell-shaped dome with $150,000 worth of gold leaf and precious stones. It is called the Shwe Dagon Pagoda.

Burma is a land of thousands of pagodas and temples. The pagodas are either round or octagonal in shape, and always an odd number of stories. Some towers rise as high as eight hundred feet. The outer walls are sometimes decorated with inscriptions from Buddhist texts, but often there are carved figures and scenes depicting the life of the Buddha or other teachers. The first Buddhist shrines were built where the ashes of Gautama Buddha had been deposited, or some other relic preserved. In Ceylon a stupa was built to enshrine what was believed to be one of his teeth.

Northern Buddhism

As India and China carried on trade with each other, the Buddha's teachings spread northward into China, Tibet, and Korea. Northern or Mahayana Buddhism has a mystical approach. As the Confucianism of the Chinese was a tolerant philosophy Buddhism met with little resistance among them. Some of the original manuscripts were taken to China and from them the Chinese version of Mahayana Buddhism developed.

Shotoku Taishi may be regarded as the founder of Japanese Buddhism. He built monasteries and dispensaries for the sick and poor, and also for animals. He wrote many commentaries on the Noble Eightfold Path.

In Buddhism those who attain enlightenment are called Bodhisattvas. These are great ones who, after reaching perfection, want to come back into physical bodies life after life until all humanity reaches perfection. One of these is said to have taken incarnation in China as Kuan-yin, the Goddess of Mercy, who watches especially over women and children. She occupies somewhat the same position in Buddhism that the Virgin Mary does in Catholic Christianity.

Statues

In his lifetime Buddha condemned idol worship, along with the caste system and superstitious rituals. However, images of him were soon being carved. This desire to carve images was probably greatly stimulated after Alexander the Great invaded Asia in the third century B.C. Some of the statues of Buddha resemble the Greek and Roman gods. Most of those found outside India, however, have Mongolian features, though Gautama was of the Aryan race that had settled in northern India. Generally the Buddha is carved in the lotus pose, with legs folded, hands relaxed on the knees, and on the face an expression of serenity and deep meditation.

There is an enormous statue of Buddha near Yokohama, which towers above the tree branches. This is over seven hundred years old, and no doubt for many generations has inspired devout Buddhists. A statue at Saranath pictures the Buddha turning the "Wheel of Life," while he explains his laws. The figure is youthful and graceful. These and other statues have helped many people understand something of the spirit of the great teacher. Similar statues may be seen all over eastern Asia. Many stone and marble cutters now make a business of carving small Buddhas for the western tourist trade.

Zen Buddhism

In 557 A.D. Bodhidharma from South India went to China and founded the Ch'an School of Buddhism that became very popular. He put less emphasis on scripture learning and more on meditation. He taught that enlightenment could come through prolonged meditation and was not obtained for one's self, but in order to help others. This cult became later known in Japan as Zen Buddhism. Since swift travel has brought the people of the world closer together, Zen Buddhism has become very popular in the West.

A western student wanting to learn something of Zen Buddhism is received cordially in the Japanese temples. When he meets the Zen Master, the student bows, touching his head to the floor. After this greeting the pupil is given instructions. He must sit on a mat in lotus fashion, which is difficult for a westerner. His hands must be relaxed and his spine erect. He is taught to breathe rhythmically and deeply. Then the pupil enters the temple where other aspirants are chanting Buddhist scriptures.

In the silence that follows, he attempts to relax his body, still his emotions and his restless mind, so that he may merge with his higher self, and in this way eventually attain enlightenment. Though stilling the active western mind is a very difficult task, many young westerners are now trying to practice this type of meditation.

Some Buddhist monks in China and Japan marry, but most live a celibate life. However, those in monasteries cannot spend all their time in meditation, so they work to raise their own food and take care of their quarters, for the begging bowl of the yellow-robed is becoming a thing of the past. Devout civilian followers of Zen in Japan rise early to meditate at their home shrines or in the temples before going to work in the cities. Then in the evening they spend another hour in meditation.

Today there are over fifty-five million Buddhists in Japan. India, which gave Buddhism to the world, now has a smaller per-cent than any other Asiatic country. In India it has become merged with Hinduism to a large extent, for the Hindus consider Gautama Buddha an *avatara,* an incarnation of Vishnu.

One of the most sacred days in the Buddhist calendar is at the time of the full moon in May, which honors the birth, enlightenment, and passing of Gautama Buddha. In the cities people wear their best clothes and place flowers in the shrines and temples. Shops and houses are also made festive, while people throng the streets in joyful moods. In some homes this is a very sacred period, when families recite the Buddha's teachings and spend the time in meditation.

Buddhism Today

As the centuries passed many sects developed out of the synthesizing of the teachings of Hinduism and Buddhism. In the towering Himalayas a sect called *Vajrayana* carved ornate statues of Shiva and Vishnu as well as Buddha. The worship of Hindu gods and the adoration of the Buddha stimulated the oriental people to the cultivation of their artistic skills in painting, sculpture, and architecture, so humanity's development was greatly advanced along these lines.

Both Hinduism and Buddhism teach the continuity of life after death, that whatsoever a man soweth that must he also reap, and that each has duties to his fellow man. While Hinduism, as understood by the simple people, developed the Godhead into many aspects that became minor gods, the Buddha taught that through meditation one could awaken the divine spark within himself and merge with the Infinite. Today this method of approach to reality is being practiced in many yoga and meditation groups in the West as well as in the East.

Though many forms of Hinduism and Buddhism have distorted the original teachings, the essence of truth which these religions proclaimed to help humanity's evolution have been treasured in their pristine glory by the most advanced of sages, who have preserved the ancient wisdom from the beginning of human development.

Suggested Further Reading:

ARNOLD, EDWIN
> *The Light of Asia,* The Theosophical Publishing House, Wheaton, Illinois, 1969 (Quest Book paperback).

BESANT, ANNIE
> *Seven Great Religions* — Buddhism. The Theosophical Publishing House, Adyar, Madras, India, 1966.

BYLES, M. B.
> *Footprints of Gautama The Buddha,* The Theosophical Publishing House, Wheaton, Illinois, 1967 (Quest Book paperback).

CONZE, E
> *Buddhism: Its Essence and Development.* Bruno Cassier, Oxford, 1957.

FRAZIER, ALLIE M.
> *Readings in Eastern Religious Thought: Buddhism,* Westminster Press, Philadelphia, 1969.

GRIMM, GEORGE
> *Doctrine of the Buddha,* Motilal Banarsidass, Delhi, India, 1965.

HUMPHREYS, CHRISTMAS
> *Buddhism,* Penguin Books, Harmonsworth, England, 1952.
> *Zen Buddhism,* Macmillan & Co., New York, 1957.

LIFE EDITORIAL STAFF
> *The World's Great Religions,* Golden Press, New York, 1967.

MORGAN, KENNETH W.
> *Path of the Buddha, The,* The Ronald Press Company, New York, 1956.

OLCOTT, HENRY S.
> *Buddhist Catechism,* The Theosophical Publishing House, Wheaton, Illinois, 1970 (Quest Book paperback).

SRI RAM, N.
> *Buddhism, Northern & Southern,* The Theosophical Publishing House, Adyar, Madras, India, 1957.

THOMAS, E. J.
> *Quest of Enlightenment,* John Murray, London (Wisdom of the East Series), 1950.

WATTS, ALAN W.
> *The Spirit of Zen,* John Murray, London, 1968.

Chapter IV

The Path of Chinese Wisdom

Taoism

China has a recorded history dating back beyond 1500 B.C. By the time her greatest sage and teacher, Confucius, was born in 551 B.C. a system of religious rituals had developed, at the core of which was ancestor worship. Ceremonies were also held and sacrifices made to the spirits of the earth, water, mountains, and weather.

During the sixth century B.C., the Chou dynasty, which had reigned for nearly eight centuries, was about to break up in the many wars between the feudal states. The peasants were overtaxed and oppressed, while the selfish, incompetent royalty ruled them. The masses were in dire need of help. As Sri Krishna had said earlier in India: "For the protection of the good, for the destruction of evildoers, for firmly establishing *dharma* (law), I am born from age to age."

So the time had come in the Divine Plan for humanity's development, for help to be sent to the Chinese people. In the sixth century B.C., China produced two great sages, whose wisdom and teachings were to guide and influence the Chinese people for nearly 2500 years.

Lao-Tse*

The first to be born, in 604 B.C., in the southern state of Chu, was Lao-tse (pronounced Loud-zuh). According to the traditions about his life, he became a very studious and wise man. In his mature years he was keeper of the Imperial Archives at Loyang, the royal capital. He advised and taught many who came to him for help. In his old age, knowing that the wickedness among the royalty was bringing about the downfall of the Chou dynasty, he decided to leave the country and take his teachings into the West. He traveled to the border on a water buffalo. There the keeper of the boundary would not let him pass until he wrote down his wise teachings for the people of China.

Lao-tse then produced a poetic work of about 500 Chinese characters, which was later called the Tao. The word *Tao* has been translated to mean "The Way of Heaven" or "Word of God." In this beautiful volume, full of gems of wisdom, Lao-tse tried to point out the path men must follow to attain perfection, just as the Buddha had taught the path of enlightenment in India. Lao-tse urged people to spend much time in "quietude" to think on spiritual ideas. He was more concerned with mysticism and the escape of the spirit from fleshly bonds than the more practical teacher, Confucius, who came after him. However Lao-tse taught many inspiring truths.

He explained that Tao means the way that must be traveled in man's climb toward a better life. Each of his verses gave his pupils much to meditate on and put into practice.

> Its name I know not, and none knows.
>   Its nature, God, I call;
> From whence all came, to which all goes —
>   The heart and home of all.
>
> Beginning's self did not begin;
>   No ending can there be.
> Who holds fast to these truths shall win
>   To immortality.

* Also spelled Lao-tze or Lao-tzu.

The symbol of Tao, representing *Yang* and *Yin*.

But who can quiet the troubled streams?
    And who can stir the stilled?
Who followed on where wisdom gleams
    Care nothing to be filled.

Who knows himself as One, no less,
    Cannot be torn apart;
Who concentrates his tenderness,
    May purify his heart.*

In addition to a way of life, Tao is also a term used for the Absolute. It is also said that Tao (Absolute) created the One and from the One came the Two with the primal and complementary forces, the *Yin* and *Yang,* out of whose constant reaction all phenomena proceeded. Yin is the passive, negative or female principle of the universe. Yang is the active, positive or male principle.

Lao-tse did not put much emphasis on rituals and ceremonies to which the people were accustomed. Though the worship of the ancient god, Chang-ti, had faded, the people observed many rituals and ceremonies connected with their worship of ancestors. They were constantly offering sacrifices and observing taboos connected with nature spirits which they believed controlled the growing of crops, flowers, storms and safety at sea.

The mystical teachings of the Tao were too abstract for the masses of the people. Deeper students and thinkers, who were advanced in their spiritual development, meditated on them and tried to put them into practice. Books were written by Chinese scholars elaborating on his teachings. The Tao has since been translated into many languages.

In his old age Lao-tse was visited by a young student named Kung-Futse, now known in the West as Confucius, who had a greater effect on the lives of the Chinese people than any other teacher. Though Lao-tse's teachings were very mystical, while those of Confucius were practical, the essential truths which the older sage taught were also at the core of Confucianism. For the eternal, unchanging, divine laws are at the heart of all religions, though these truths are often later distorted and misinterpreted.

In the sixth century B.C. which produced Lao-tse and Confucius, there was a great spiritual upsurge in all the civilized world. Buddha was teaching in India; Pythagoras, the great mathe-

* *Tao,* Charles H. Mackintosh.

matician and philosopher, had his school of wisdom in Greece; Zoroaster, in Persia, was teaching of the one Supreme Being, Ahura-Mazda, and his message of fire in all beings; and Isaiah, over a century earlier, had written his prophecy for the Hebrew people, foretelling the coming of another great teacher, Jesus.

Ancestor Worship

For centuries before the coming of Lao-tse and Confucius the Chinese people had practiced ancestor worship. They believed that man's surest immortality was in the memory of his descendants and the continuity of his name in history. Every home had its shrine, of one sort and another, to the memory of the departed. In poorer homes this might be only a small box in which the family kept the names of their ancestors. On birthdays or other special days these were honored by reciting their virtues, and making offerings of food or flowers at the shrine.

Through these practices the Chinese people developed pride of family and strong bonds of affection that held large groups of people together as a unit. This laid the foundation for a nation that has endured as an entity longer than any other in the world.

The happiest grandfather was one who had several generations living around one courtyard. There were strong bonds among the individuals. Gentle courtesy and respect for the aged was at the core of family life. Earnings were shared for the common good. If one member of the family was ill or in trouble, all rallied to his aid. All cooperated in trying to give a good education to those who were studious and bright. Thus ancestor worship and strong family bonds held the people of China together for many centuries.

Confucianism

Confucius, whose teachings gave the Chinese people new direction, was born 551 B.C. in Ch'u Fu in northeast China near Shantung. Many years later when the Jesuit priests entered China his real name, Kung Fu-tse, was given the Latin pronunciation, Confucius, by which he is now known around the world.

According to tradition Kung Fu-tse's father was Shu Liang Ho, though he was generally called Kung the Tall. He was a giant of a man, about seven feet tall. He longed for a son to carry on the Kung name. However, his wife presented him with nine daughters in succession and no sons. Kung gave up hope when he was seventy and divorced her to marry a sixteen year old girl, Yen Chentsai.

Kung and Yen went to Mount Mu, China's most sacred mountain to pray for a son. A few months later, tradition claims, Yen dreamed she would have a son, just as Gautama Buddha's birth was foretold to his mother in a dream, and Mary in Palestine was told by an angel of the coming of Jesus.

The future sage, Kung Fu-tse, grew to be a very large and remarkable child. By the time he was six he had learned the temple rituals and played at observing them with his friends. His fondness for rituals and ceremonies continued throughout his life. He grew to be taller than his father. His eyes were opened wider than those of the average Chinese, and his ears were unusually large, a fact which people considered a mark of great intelligence.

Kung the Tall lived only a few years after his son was born, so Yen Chentsai left the home where Kung's first wife and nine daughters still lived, and went to live with a more prosperous kinsman. There the competent young woman brought up her son under strict discipline. She was very careful about his clothes, his cleanliness, and daily habits. Though there were no public schools she gave him the best education the times afforded, for he was an excellent student and loved study.

By the age of seventeen the young man had acquired such a reputation for intelligence, industry, and honesty, that he secured a position keeping the granary accounts for the wealthy Chi family in the state of Lu. But young Kung found no intellectual satisfaction in collecting taxes from the poor peasants.

When he was nineteen his mother selected a wife for him from the state of Sung. Tradition claims that Kung Fu-tse's strict ritual of living was so exacting that life must have been difficult for his wife. But marriage was necessary to continue the ancient Kung name through his sons. Kung Li was born a year later, but was generally called Po Yu. From him has descended a long line of Kungs to the present generation. Later one of the descendants was made a duke, so there is said to be a Duke Kung still living in China.

Confucius became a teacher when he was twenty-two. A year later, after his mother died, he retired temporarily from public life and spent the next three years in mourning for her, as was the traditional custom. Much of this time was occupied in study of the history of China. Soon after that Confucius became very much interested in music and studied under a famous musician, Hsiang. He said that music helped one understand the harmony of the universe.

When Confucius was about thirty-three years old, the son of a powerful minister of Lu was sent to study under him. This brought the Master new prestige and more pupils. When his disciples asked questions, he tried to make them think out the answers for themselves.

He took a trip to the capital, Loyang, and visited the temples dedicated to Heaven and Earth, where he delighted in the rituals and the music. But more than all else he wanted to talk with the famous teacher, Lao-tse. According to tradition, the two great thinkers, who were trying to teach people in different ways, had a long conversation in which Confucius praised the ancient teachers of the Chinese. Lao-tse advised him to put away the past, stating that people should live in the present. However many of Lao-tse's pupils preferred to live the lives of hermits, spending most of their time in study and deep meditation. The teachings of Confucius on the other hand, were more practical. He encouraged people to know the glory of China's past, and emulate its finest traditions in developing better citizens and better government.

His teachings were easier than those of Lao-tse for the average person to put into practice. He always laid great stress on sincerity in such sayings as:

> Take conscientiousness and sincerity as your ruling principles, submit also your mind to right conditions, and your character will improve. [1]

Again on improving character he said:

> If a man put duty first and success after, will not that improve his character? If he attack his own failings instead of those of others, will he not remedy his personal faults? [2]

He advised them to have a definite purpose in life, and tried to show them how to attain it:

[1] *The Analects,* Chap. X, 1
[2] *The Analects,* Chap. XXI, 2

Only when one knows where one is to rest can one have a fixed purpose. Only with a fixed purpose can one achieve calmness of mind. Only with calmness of mind can one attain a tranquil repose. Only in a tranquil repose can one devote oneself to careful deliberation. Only through careful deliberation can one attain the highest good.[1]

Thus in the details of his teachings he tried to encourage and instruct the people on how to attain the highest good, or that perfection about which others also taught. About five hundred years later when the Buddhist teachings began to mingle with Confucianism, the people could more readily understand that this perfection could not be attained in one life, but through a succession of lives in which the necessary lessons are learned and the path of spiritual development trod in different races under more and more evolved teachers.

Five hundred years later the Christ in Palestine also laid emphasis on this attainment when he said:

Be ye therefore perfect, even as your Father which is in heaven is perfect.[2]

When Confucius was about fifty, he became Chief Justice for Duke Ting in the state of Lu. So effective were his teachings and his administration of the courts that crime practically disappeared from Lu. But the Duke of the bordering state became jealous of Duke Ting's thriving kingdom and schemed to entice him away from his virtuous living that had set such a good example for his people.

He sent Duke Ting a gift of beautiful dancing girls and fine horses. So charmed was the Duke that he took the girls into his harem and began to live a dissolute life, neglecting his rituals and ceremonies. Completely frustrated, Confucius resigned his post and went into exile with some of his faithful disciples.

The Master wandered from state to state, hoping to find a ruler who would put his precepts concerning good government into practice. No ruler wanted to give up his selfish, easy habits to practice the austerities of this wandering teacher. No one wanted to listen to such advice as:

Govern the people by laws and regulate them by penalties, and the people will try to do no wrong, but they will lose

[1] *The Sacred Books of Confucius*
[2] Matthew: 5:48

the sense of shame. Govern the people by virtue and restrain them by rules of propriety, and the people will have a sense of shame and be reformed of themselves.[1]

Confucius was sixty-eight when he was finally called back to the state of Lu. He no longer wanted public office, but with a few of his most learned disciples he edited and wrote a number of books. He had always been a deep student and lover of Chinese history and the wisdom of its great sages. He arranged and edited music for the temple and the court ceremonies. He edited several books, which for centuries have been Chinese classics: *The Book of History; The Book of Poetry; The Book of Ceremony;* and *The Book of Changes*. He also wrote a brief history of the state of Lu. *The Analects,* the volume of his teachings best known in the West, is a collection of his sayings during conversations with his pupils, in which they discussed character building, virtue, courtesy, self-discipline, and the duties of those who govern. They were probably compiled by pupils of two of Confucius' disciples, Yseng and Yu, and have since been translated into many languages.

In *The Analects* the Master spoke often of character:

The man of honour thinks often of his character, the inferior man of his position. The man of honour desires justice, the inferior man favour.[2]

When questioned about teachers Confucius said:

He first practices what he preaches and afterwards preaches what he practices.[3]

He spoke much about good government and honorable rulers, who could inspire people to better living by their examples:

He who governs by his moral excellence may be compared to the pole-star, which abides in its place, while all the stars bow towards it.[4]

The Analects became one of the four books which helped shape the Chinese character and further its development. Other books were written by disciples of the old Master — *Great Learning, Doctrine of Man,* and *Mencius*.

[1] *The Sacred Books of Confucius*
[2] *The Analects*
[3] *The Analects*
[4] *The Analects*

A Chinese priest teaching his pupil the ethics of Confucius.

Photograph by A. Devaney, Inc., N. Y.

Confucius had often said that royal birth did not necessarily fit a man for public office, but that those holding government positions should be chosen for character and ability. Over two centuries after the death of Confucius, during the Han dynasty, his teachings became the basis for training public officials. Everyone seeking government office had to stand an examination on the Confucian classics, thus raising the standards of Chinese life.

Confucius' son, Po Lu, died soon after the old man returned to Lu. When Po Lu's son, Chi, became older he was a student of Confucianism under the old Master's disciple Tseng Tzu. He eventually became one of the most learned and ardent of his grandfather's disciples.

Five years after returning to his native Lu, Confucius died in his family home at Ch'u Fu in 479 B.C. at the age of 73. His tomb is visited by thousands of devotees and pilgrims each year. About two hundred and fifty years after his passing, the head of the Han dynasty offered an ox in sacrifice at his tomb, so the custom of an annual sacrifice was kept up for many centuries.

About five hundred years after the death of Confucius, Buddhist missionaries arrived in China, bringing with them the teachings of cause and effect, rebirth, and knowledge of the divine Hierarchy, which sends teachers to help humanity from time to time. This more mystical religion seemed to fill a gap in the philosophical teachings of Confucius, and in some ways it harmonized with the Taoism of Lao-tse. Many Chinese mingled the three and considered themselves followers of Confucianism, Buddhism, and Taoism, so that today shrines, images, pagodas, and temples of all three faiths are found in China.

These faiths helped develop the character of the Chinese people through many centuries, but they faded somewhat with the establishment of the Chinese Republic in 1911, and after the Christian missionaries were allowed to enter China.

Confucianism has passed through many changes over the centuries. At one time an emperor ordered all the books burned. Some were hidden and preserved, among them copies of *The Analects,* one of which was found in the wall of Confucius' old home in Lu. Eventually people began to think of Confucius as a god and built temples to him all over the country. Sacrifices were made to him and many superstitious practices developed. Often the original teachings of the sage were distorted by various interpretations, in the same way that the original teachings of the Buddha and Jesus have been understood differently, so that these faiths are now divided into many sects and denominations.

Though Confucius did not profess to know much about the after-life and the nature of the Divine Creator, his moral and ethical teachings gave a great impetus to the moral and spiritual development of the Chinese people. He is justly acclaimed as one of the great sages of the world, who came at a crucial time to help humanity on its upward path toward the goal of perfection. Attempts of Confucius to restore a feudal system failed under pressure of western ideas, but his ethical codes for individuals and society, based on eternal truths, have been a vital force in shaping the character and destinies of the Chinese people.

Unlike Hinduism and Buddhism, Confucianism did not spread widely beyond the boundaries of China, and later Taiwan. Before the Communist regime, it was estimated that there were about 340 million followers of Lao-tse and Confucius. However under Communist dictatorship many of the old temples, shrines, and images have been destroyed and religion has been discouraged. Lao-tse and Confucius served a great purpose in the Divine Plan for humanity by their ethical and moral teachings, which fitted the needs of the Chinese people.

Suggested Further Reading:

CHAN, WING-TSIT
    A Source Book in Chinese Philosophy, Princeton University Press, Princeton, New Jersey, 1963.

CH'U CHAI and WINDBERG CHAI
    The Sacred Books of Confucius, University House, New York, 1965.

CROW, CARL
    Master Kung, Harper & Bros., New York, 1938.

DE BARY, WM. THEODORE, CHAN, WING-TSIT, and
WATSON, BURTON
    Sources of Chinese Tradition, vols. 1-2, Princeton University Press, Princeton, New Jersey, 1969.

DE REINCOURT, AMSURY
    The Soul of China, Coward-McCann, New York, 1958.

GILES, MURIEL
    The Sayings of Confucius, John Murray, London, 1969 (Wisdom of the East Series).

    The Sayings of Lao Tzu, John Murray, London, 1950 (Wisdom of the East Series).

JASPER, CARL
    The Great Philosophers, Harcourt, Brace & World, New York, 1957.

LATOURETTE, KENNETH SCOTT
    The Chinese, Their History & Culture, The Macmillan Co., New York, 1934.

LI, DUN J.
    The Ageless Chinese, Scribners, New York, 1965.

LIFE EDITORIAL STAFF
    The World's Great Religions, Golden Press, New York, 1967.

LIN YUTANG
    The Wisdom of Confucius, Random House, New York, 1943.

    The Wisdom of Laotse, Modern Library, New York, 1968.

MACKINTOSH, CHARLES H.
    Tao, The Theosophical Publishing House, Wheaton, Ill. 1926.

MOORE, CHARLES A.
    The Chinese Mind, East-West Center, University of Hawaii Press, Honolulu, 1967.

SEEGAR, ELIZABETH
    The Pageant of Chinese History, Longmans, Green & Co., New York, 1947.

WALEY, ARTHUR
    The Analects of Confucius, George Allen & Unwin, London, 1964.

    Three Ways of Thought in Ancient China, George Allen & Unwin, London, 1963.

LET THERE BE LIGHT

Temple Emanu-el Community Center, Lynbrook, New York. The seven-branched candlestick or Menorah is the emblem most frequently found in Jewish art and culture. It is one of the most important appurtenances of the synagogue.

Photograph by A. Devaney, Inc., N. Y.

Chapter V

The Path of Judaism

Abraham

While Indian sages were teaching the earliest Vedas of the Hindu faith, and long before Gautama Buddha or Confucius, Abraham was born in Ur of Chaldea. This man, through his belief in one God, was destined to become the fountainhead to which three great religions trace their source. The events of his life are recorded in the Old Testament, which is now a part of the religious scriptures of Judaism, Christianity, and Islam.

Traditions tell a colorful story of why Abraham left his home in Chaldea for the Promised Land. He was the son of Terah, a shepherd and idol maker. Sometimes young Abraham helped his father make images of clay and stone to sell. Often, too, he watched sheep by day and slept in the open at night. Eventually he revolted against worshiping idols he had made with his own hands. Meditating under the canopy of stars at night he eventually came to the conclusion that there could be only one overall power, a God not made with hands.

When he destroyed the images in the shop and proclaimed a

God of the spirit, the idol worshipers turned against him. So Terah took his son Abraham and his wife, Sarah, and the rest of the family and set out for the new land God had promised them. After Terah died on the westward journey God spoke to Abraham in a vision:

> Get thee out of thy country . . . unto a land that I will show thee. And I will make of thee a great nation.[1]

The families multiplied and soon became a tribe as they fought against other tribes on their way to the Promised Land. After reaching Canaan, threatened starvation drove them to the fertile valley of the Nile in Egypt, but eventually they returned to Canaan. During all these struggles Abraham had constant dreams and visions in which he received instructions and encouragement from God:

> Fear not, Abram, I am thy shield; and thy exceeding great reward. . . . Look now toward the heaven, and tell the stars, if thou be able to number them; and he said unto him, so shall thy seed be.[2]

Abraham could not understand this prophecy, for his wife, Sarah, had borne him no children. After he discussed it with her, she suggested that he have an heir by her slave, Hagar, whom she had brought from Egypt. This son was named Ishmael. But some time later, in her old age, Sarah had a son, Isaac. When Hagar proudly assumed that her son, Ishmael, would be his father's heir, Sarah wanted Abraham to banish her and the child into the desert.

Abraham was deeply distressed, but again God came to him in a vision and said:

> Abraham, let it not be grievous in thy sight because of the lad, and because of thy bondwoman; in all that Sarah hath said unto thee, hearken unto her voice; for in Isaac shall thy seed be called. And also of the son of thy bondwoman will I make a great nation, because of thy seed.[3]

So Hagar and Ishmael were banished and traveled southward toward Egypt. There Ishmael eventually married an Egyptian and became the source from which the Arab nation sprang that eventually gave the world the religion of Islam.

[1] Genesis 12:1,2
[2] Genesis 15:1,5
[3] Genesis 21:12,13

60

After Abraham's death Isaac became the patriarch of his people and the ancestor of a long line of rulers, teachers, and prophets. Isaac had two sons, Jacob and Esau. Jacob had twelve sons from whom the twelve tribes of Israel descended. The Pentateuch (first five books of the Bible) tells the colorful story of their adventures, which are familiar to Jews, Christians, and Muslims.

Moses

The actual beginning of a clearly defined religion, with rules and rituals, dates back to Moses somewhere between 1400 and 1200 B.C. This law-giver of Judaism was born in Egypt while the Israelites were held in bondage there. According to the account in Exodus, Pharaoh ordered that all male children under two years old among the Israelites should be slain. Hoping to save her child's life, Moses' mother hid him near a stream where he was rescued by Pharaoh's daughter and brought up in the royal palace. This story of the rescue of an infant, destined to become a great teacher, is found in the lore of Hinduism, Judaism, and Christianity as well as in other mythical traditions.

The great spiritual awareness which Moses later displayed, seems to indicate that he had been educated by the Egyptian priests at the court of Pharaoh. Challenged by the suffering of his enslaved people, Moses eventually led them out of Egypt and across the Sinai desert. On reaching the craggy mountain named Yehovh (Jehovah), now called Mount Sinai, Moses dedicated his people to the worship of this one God, Jehovah. He was regarded as their tribal God, while other tribes had their own gods.

After spending forty days on the mountain, Moses brought down the tablets on which he had written the Ten Commandments God had given him.*

THE TEN COMMANDMENTS

I am the Lord thy God. . . . Thou shalt have no other gods before me.

Thou shalt not make unto thee any graven image, or any likeness of anything that is in heaven above, or that is in the

* Exodus 20:1-17

61

earth beneath. . . . Thou shalt not bow down thyself to them, nor serve them. . . .

Thou shalt not take the name of the Lord thy God in vain. . . .

Remember the sabbath day to keep it holy. Six days shalt thou labor and do all thy work. . . .

Honor thy father and thy mother that thy days may be long upon the land which the Lord thy God giveth thee.

Thou shalt not kill.

Thou shalt not commit adultery.

Thou shalt not steal.

Thou shalt not bear false witness against thy neighbor.

Thou shalt not covet.

The commandments are negatively given, indicating what not to do, with consequences following. Four of them concern man's duty to God, six his duty to his fellow man. In later centuries Jesus, who knew the Hebrew scriptures, expressed these commandments briefly in one sentence:

Thou shalt love the Lord thy God with all thy heart, and with all thy soul, and with all thy strength, and with all thy mind; and thy neighbor as thyself.*

The ten commandments were first given in Exodus, then again in Deuteronomy toward the end of the Israelite wanderings in the desert. The difference in wording of those two passages indicates that they were passed down by word of mouth. Most of the Israelites, who had escaped from bondage in Egypt, had by then passed on, so it was a younger generation that had to fight its way to the Promised Land.

In addition to the ten commandments, Moses gave specific instructions for building the tabernacle in the desert, with detailed instructions about the candelabra, vessels for ritualistic services, and other details. Many of the strict laws of sanitation, concerning the preparing of food, were necessary at the time in the desert where there was no refrigeration. The people were also given instruction about circumcision, which distinguished them from all other people, until medical science discovered its value as a pre-

* Luke 10:27

caution against disease. Now it has become almost a universal practice.

Few at that time understood the inner significance of the rituals as means of tuning themselves in to the infinite source of being. Most obeyed them because Moses had given them as God's laws, so they made some progress spiritually through the discipline.

The Ark of the Covenant

Moses had married the daughter of the chief priest of the Kenites. She worshiped the God, Yahovh, or Jehovah, who was said to dwell on Mt. Sinai. Moses and his people entered into a covenant with Jehovah that he would protect them as long as they kept his commandments.

Moses received instructions from Jehovah about how to build the ark, as a sacred receptacle for their covenant. At that time the Israelites were somewhat like the present-day Bedouin tribes of the Arabian Desert, continually at war with neighboring tribes and often among themselves. The ark went before them as a shield in battle, for they believed that their god was greater than the gods of other tribes, against whom they fought on their way to the Promised Land. These battles were symbolic also of the struggle of these primitive people to conquer their lower natures and live by the higher principles which Moses had pointed out to them.

A detailed description of the ark is given in Chapter 37 of Exodus. It was made of a yellowish-brown wood that grew in the mountains, and was covered and lined with gold. Four golden rings at the corners held poles for carrying. Mounted on top were two cherubim facing each other. This seems to indicate that the Israelites believed in a hierarchy of angelic hosts, as did the Far Eastern peoples, though these invisible helpers were called by different names. To the simple people of the desert, the ark was the evidence of the "house of God." God was said to dwell between the cherubim.

Centuries later, after the Israelites were established in the Promised Land, Solomon's Temple was built to house the ark of the Covenant and for a place of worship.

Thus were these tough and warlike people of the desert brought under rigid discipline that was destined to train them through God's commandments, under the dedicated leadership of Moses and Aaron, his brother, in reverence for God and consideration for their fellow men.

The Jehovah which these early Israelites worshiped seemed modeled after their own stage of development. He not only led them in battle, but could be ruthless toward their enemies, or any of the Israelites who broke his laws. There was more fear and awe in their attitude toward him than adoration and love. But the fear of suffering the consequences of Jehovah's wrath was a restraining influence to the impetuous men of that era. They made slow but steady progress in discrimination and the control of desires and actions.

After wandering for forty years in the desert, the Israelites finally came within sight of the Promised Land. For those able to understand the inner meanings of religious scriptures, forty is a significant number. Moses was forty days on Mt. Sinai and led his people for forty years through the wilderness. Gautama Buddha meditated for forty days before gaining Enlightenment or Buddhahood, and later Jesus spent forty days and nights in the wilderness, at the end of which time he resisted the temptations and attained "at-oneness" with the Christ. For those who seek to live by the spirit of the teachings of any religion, rather than by the letter of the law, meditation on these inner meanings can be an illuminating experience.

Moses himself never entered the Promised Land, in spite of his long struggle to bring the Israelites through "the wilderness of sin" (Exodus 17:11). Though he was no doubt more spiritually evolved than his followers, he had offended Jehovah while in a rage on finding his people bowing to a golden calf and had destroyed the tablets on which the commandments were written. He was permitted only to view the fertile valley of the Jordan from a mountain top before he died.

A younger generation eventually conquered the Canaanites and settled among them to become an agricultural as well as a pastoral people. Many were tempted to worship the god of the Canaanites, Baal. As Baal was god of the soil, it was believed that his favor must be sought for good harvests, so some of the Israelites were soon including this god in their worship. Many of the festivals and seasonal rites of Baal were gradually incorporated into the worship of Jehovah. But slowly as the people developed, and, centuries later, in the time of the prophets, he was portrayed as a kind, forgiving, and loving father. Even in the earlier days the idea of a universal creator had come to Jacob after his vision, in a strange land, of angels ascending and descending a ladder to heaven, for he exclaimed, "Surely the Lord is in this place and I knew it not." [1]

Hebrew Scriptures

The history and religion of the Jewish people are interwoven. Their sacred books record the development of both. Most of their scriptures were written in Hebrew. The emphasis was on helping people live a good life here on earth, according to God's instructions. The ultimate aim was man's perfection. So had the Buddha tried to teach his people how to attain enlightenment or perfection. As in other living religions, the keynotes of Judaism were man's reverence for his Creator and his duty toward his brothers.

The composition of the books which make up the Old Testament covered a period from about 1200 B.C. until the second century B.C. The Hebrew text comprised twenty-four documents, arranged in three parts: the law, or *Torah,* containing the first five books of the Bible; the Prophets; and the Writings. In the King James version that part which Christians call the Old Testament contains thirty-nine books.

In the *Torah* are Genesis, Exodus, Leviticus, Numbers, and Deuteronomy. Genesis begins with the story of creation, in which, no doubt, days represent eras in the world's physical evolution. There are also the allegorical stories of Adam and Noah, and the flood stories, slightly different, but basically similar to those found in other religious literature. Then the account goes on to Abraham's belief in one God, which is Judaism's great contribution to the religious development of the world:

> The Lord appeared to Abram, and said unto him, I am the Almighty God; walk before me, and be thou perfect. [2]

Although the *Torah* is said to have been written by Moses, this seems impossible as it contains an account of his death. However it is an amazing record of what he did for the Israelites and

[1] Genesis 28:15
[2] Genesis 17:1

A boy places the bell-hung crowns over the Torah Scrolls during a synagogue service. The crown, the lion, and the tablets embroidered on the
Torah cover are traditional Jewish symbols.

the spiritual development of a great people. He emphasized strongly that men must learn the laws of their physical, emotional, mental, and spiritual being, and suffer the results if they break these laws. The teachers of the East had tried to impress their followers with the same truth, and had called this law of cause and effect, *karma*.

The books of the prophets bring the history of the Jews and their religion to about 586 B.C. The most inspiring writings of the soul's struggle to attain God-consciousness may be found in the books of Isaiah, Ezekiel, Kings, etc. These books describe the many stages of spiritual growth through which the people passed.

In the great poetic writings such as the Psalms of David the spark of God slowly awakening within the human soul was fanned to flame by his comforting words:

> If I take the wings of the morning, and dwell in the uttermost parts of the sea;
> Even there shall thy hand lead me, and thy right hand shall hold me.[1]

Surely this God of David had become a universal God, not a tribal Jehovah. In this atomic age the immensity of the Almighty seems more stupendous and awe-inspiring than ever! David, the king and poet, caught a glimpse of this immensity when he wrote:

> The heavens declare the glory of God; and the firmament sheweth his handiwork.[2]

While in captivity in Babylon the prophet Ezekiel reminded his people that their bondage was punishment for their unrighteousness and broken laws, for too often they had bowed down and worshiped the idols of the people among whom they lived.

Hosea tried to do away with some of the bloody, pagan rites the children of Israel had practiced in the wilderness and afterward, when he wrote:

> For I desired mercy, and not sacrifice; and the knowledge of God, more than burnt offerings.[3]

All this represents tremendous spiritual growth under the leadership of inspired teachers. Those who wrote these scriptures

[1] Psalms 139:9,10
[2] Psalms 19:1
[3] Hosea 6:6

were the teachers and prophets who had attained a spiritual station higher than the average, for most people still observed the letter of the law rather than the spirit.

The books which now comprise the Old Testament were completed before the time of Jesus, but were not compiled until the first century A.D. In the meantime commentaries had been written on the various scriptures. These were eventually gathered into a collection called the *Talmud*. The *Talmud* is used today by scholars and rabbis. The *Kabalah* is a collection of writings used by those who delve even deeper into the hidden meanings of the scriptures. It deals with the essential truths of Judaism — truths which are at the core of all living religions — and points out how each is suited to the period of human evolution and the type of people to whom it was given.

It has been said that the average man goes to the *Torah* and the prophets for help, learned men study the *Talmud,* and the wise meditate on the *Kabalah*.

At the beginning of the Christian era the Jews were divided into sects: the Pharisees, Sadducees, and Essenes. The Pharisees believed they had a right to interpret the scriptures in their own way and added many new laws. Unlike the Sadducees they believed in life after death and the angelic hosts. The Pharisees were the champions of the common people, while the Sadducees were the wealthier, ruling class. As a result of these conflicting beliefs, enmity sprang up between the two groups.

The third sect, the Essenes, was a secret organization. This mystical group of people interpreted and lived by the inner meaning of the scriptures. It is believed that they dwelt near where the Dead Sea Scrolls were found in the twentieth century. Tradition says that some of their teachings were so secret that they were not committed to writing, but passed down from teacher to pupil through glyphs and symbols, so that the uninitiated could not understand them. In the hands of the selfish and worldly, this knowledge could have been used to gain power over others, so it was kept secret. Some of the teachings were, however, committed to writing in the Middle Ages and are now known as the *Kabalah*. Some claim that Jesus was taught by the Essenes between his twelfth and thirtieth years, after he displayed such wisdom to the rabbis in the temple when a boy.

Jewish Holy Days and Festivals

The most holy day of the Jews is the Sabbath, which begins at sundown on Friday, and ends when the first stars twinkle out on Saturday. Sabbath is the English translation of the Hebrew word, *Shabbat,* which means rest. Orthodox Jews observe the Sabbath strictly according to Mosaic laws.

They do no work or cooking on the Sabbath, nor do they travel in modern conveyances, but walk to the synagogue. Nor will they telephone, write letters, buy, or sell. It is strictly a day of rest and prayers.

On the Sabbath evening the father of the family attends a service at the synagogue before going home for a special supper. His wife has set the table with the best linen and china. When the family gathers she lights the ceremonial candles. Then the family says:

> Blessed art thou, O Lord our God, King of the Universe, who hath sanctified us by Thy law and commandments to kindle the Sabbath light.

The mother of the family has observed the strict dietary laws of Moses. No pork or shell fish is eaten, nor are dairy products served in the same vessels used for meat. The wine and specially-made bread are passed to all the family. The eating of white bread on the Sabbath is a custom brought down from the time when the Jews had only dark bread during the week and saved the scarce white bread for the Sabbath feast.

When the opening ritual of the bread and wine is complete all say together in Hebrew, *Shabbat shalom,* which means "Sabbath peace to you."

For all Jews the Sabbath is a pleasant day of relaxation, when there is time for discussing the sacred scriptures and turning one's thoughts to God. Conservative and Reform Jews do not observe all the Mosaic laws as strictly as do the Orthodox. Most Jews hold their main service in synagogues and temples on Friday evening, followed by a social hour with religious study and other services on the Sabbath morning.

Christians and Muslims also use the Old Testament as part of their sacred scriptures and observe the rest day, which Christians observe on Sunday, and Muslims observe on Friday.

New Year

The beginning of the Jewish New Year is not on January first, but in the seventh lunar month thereafter. In the Hebrew calendar the first of each month comes at the time of the new moon. This makes their New Year come some time in the fall, in September or October. In the old days in Palestine this was harvest time with a harvest festival, when grapes, wheat, and other products were gathered. People took stock of the past year and looked to the future with better resolutions.

The first day is called *Rosh Hashanah,* which means "beginning of the year." The celebration continues for ten days. During the first meal on *Rosh Hashanah* a blessing is asked and thanks given for all the good things of the year.

Different countries and religious groups celebrate New Year at various times — Christians on January first, Jews in the fall. The Hindus also celebrate their New Year in the fall at a Festival of Light, called *Divali.* For all it is a time for checking business accounts, examining past character failures, and making better resolutions for the future.

The Jewish celebration is ushered in by blowing the *shofar* or ram's horn, which has traditional significance. Moses had the *shofar* blown at the foot of Mount Sinai to gather the people together to hear the Ten Commandments for the first time. In the centuries that followed before the Romans drove the Jews from Palestine, it was blown to announce the beginning of the Sabbath and other holy days.

The last day of the Jewish New Year is called *Yom Kippur.* *Yom* means day, and *Kippur,* atonement or cleansing from sin. This is the day of fasting and prayer when people examine their weaknesses and try to return to union with God. This is the high, most holy day when the soul-stirring music of *Kol Nidre* is heard in the synagogues. The words now used originated in the anguished cry to God from the persecuted Jews of Spain during the Inquisition. The Jews there were forced to pretend they were converted to Roman Catholicism, or face death or banishment. Those who pretended to accept the new religion secretly continued to worship in their own way. On the Day of Atonement they chanted three times in Hebrew their plaintive appeal to God for forgiveness:

70

All vows, bonds, devotions, promises, obligations, penalties, and oaths; wherewith we have vowed, sworn, devoted and bound ourselves; from this Day of Atonement unto the next Day of Atonement, may it come unto us for good; lo, all these, we repent us in them. They shall be absolved, released, annulled, made void and of none effect; they shall not be binding nor shall they have any power. Our vows shall not be vows, our bonds shall not be bonds; and our oaths shall not be oaths.*

Another important observation among the Jews is the *Passover.* This begins at the time of the first full moon in the spring. It commemorates events just before the Israelites' flight from Egypt when an angel passed over the homes of Jewish children, whom Pharaoh had ordered killed.

For centuries the Jewish prophets had written of a Messiah or Redeemer who would come and set up an earthly kingdom for them. Christians believe he did come as Jesus Christ. The Last Supper of Jesus was a Passover celebration. However the Jews are still looking for a Messiah.

Another celebration, *Sukkoth,* is observed at harvest time, five days after *Yom Kippur. Sukkoth* was the forerunner of the American Thanksgiving. This festival was a gay time when Jews thanked God, not only for the harvest but also for the *Torah.*

Hanukkah is an eight-day celebration in December, dramatizing the period when the Jews freed themselves from the rule of a Syrian king, and drove the idol worshipers from the temple. This is called the Feast of Lights. On the opening night of *Hanukkah* one candle is lighted in a candelabra holding eight. Each night thereafter another candle is lighted until there are eight burning. Traditions say that after the temple was cleared of idol worshipers, the Jews could find only enough oil to burn in the temple for one night. However, the oil continued to burn for eight nights. In memory of this, eight candles are burned in Jewish homes during *Hanukkah.* Special foods are served during this celebration. Among some of the people, presents are given children each night, with the best saved for the eighth night.

Thus through observance of many holy days, the Jews have kept alive the history of their people and their religion. This has

* *Synagogue Service;* New Year and Atonement (Orthodox), Hebrew Publishing Co., New York, p. 15, in Service for Day of Atonement.

made of them a closely-knit group of people under one God, to whom the majority have given homage through the centuries of struggle, captivity, conquest, and persecution.

As their dramatic story is followed through the Old Testament, we find the peak of their glory as a nation came about the time of King David and his son Solomon. During the latter's reign, the great temple of Solomon was built in Jerusalem for worship and to house the Ark of the Covenant.

There was continual struggle between the idol-worshiping neighbors and conquerors and these people, who worshiped one God. When in captivity, many succumbed to the lure of the flesh, the worship of idols, and gods of nature. But always there were the teachers and prophets to exhort them to turn back to the worship of one God. Their writings have since given inspiration to millions of Jews and many people of other faiths on their upward path toward a oneness in consciousness with God, for the truths they taught are at the core of all living religions.

Later History

Finally, in 63 B.C., the Romans occupied the Holy Land. In 70 A.D. Solomon's Temple was destroyed by the conquerors and the Jews were driven out of Jerusalem. Many were already scattered over Europe, North Africa, and the Far East. But wherever they went they clung secretly to their belief in one God, the Mosaic laws, and the rituals they had always observed. The persecutions, intended to crush them, only disciplined them and challenged them to excel intellectually and in many skills. All over the world their people have attained the highest peaks in industry, the arts, religion, finances, and politics.

Today, in the observance of their religious rites, there are three groups in Judaism. The Orthodox still observe strictly the Mosaic Laws as given by Moses in the desert. This includes following the old dietary laws which were so necessary in 1400 B.C. in the tropical desert when there was no refrigeration for the preservation of food. Conservative Jews have relaxed some of these rigid laws, but are not so free in their observance of some of the laws and rituals as are the Reformed Jews. Orthodox Jews have their own synagogues, while Reformed Jews generally call their places of worship temples.

The heartless slaughter of millions of Jews during Hitler's regime in Europe is the darkest blot on human history. Reaction came promptly in awakened understanding and sympathy for a cruelly oppressed people. The Zionist movement had already been started among the Jews, and with the newly-aroused compassion among people of all faiths, the United Nations, in 1947, created a national refuge for the Jews on their old home site. Many thousands of Jews have since settled in Israel. Though Judaism is not the state religion, many there still live by the old religion. Others, who do not, are free to live according to their own beliefs. Sadly enough the old enmity between the Arab descendants of Ishmael and his brother Isaac's Jewish people has flared again.

Today there are more than 13 million Jews living all over the world, with almost half of them in North and South America, where there is no actual religious persecution. As in all other religions, some Jews are pious and very devoted to their faith. Some are regular in attendance at services; others are not. All are free to choose whether they will observe the strict rules and regulations of the Orthodox faith or adopt Reformed Judaism. But all still follow the religion of the one God. This is their great contribution to man's spiritual evolution, while their religious scriptures became the foundation out of which the teachings of Christianity and Islam developed.

Suggested Further Reading:

The Old Testament of the Bible.

BROWNE, LEWIS
This Believing World, The Macmillan Co., New York, 1961.

FITCH, FLORENCE MARY
One God, Lothrop, Lee & Shepard, New York, 1954.

FORTUNE, DION
The Mystical Qabalah, Williams & Norgate, Ltd., London, 1948.

GAER, JOSEPH
How the Great Religions Began, Dodd, Mead & Co., New York, 1957.
Love of the Old Testament, Grosset & Dunlap, Inc., New York.

HALL, MANLY
How to Understand Your Bible (Old and New Testaments), Philosophical Research Society, Los Angeles, 1942.

HERTZBERG, ARTHUR
Judaism, Washington Square Press, New York, 1962 (paperback).

HODSON, GEOFFREY
The Hidden Wisdom in the Holy Bible, Vol. 2, The Theosophical Publishing House, Wheaton, Illinois, 1969 (Quest Book paperback).

HUME, ROBERT M.
The World's Great Religions, Scribner's, New York, 1959.

KRITZECK, JAMES
Sons of Abraham, Helicon Press, Baltimore, 1965.

LIFE EDITORIAL STAFF
The World's Great Religions, Golden Press, New York, 1967.

MORROW, BETTY & LOUIS
Jewish Holidays, Garrard, Champaign, Illinois, 1967.

SYNAGOGUE SERVICE NEW YEAR AND ATONEMENT
Hebrew Publishing Co., New York.

Chapter VI

The Path of Christianity

Jesus

As the conquests of the Roman emperors brought to an end the Jewish rule in Palestine, the time had come for the ages-old divine truths to be given to the world in a new form to inspire civilizations yet to be developed in Europe and the Americas. Humanity's spiritual development must go on to greater heights as man evolves in body, emotions, mind, and soul.

For eight centuries before the Christian era, Jewish prophets had been predicting the coming of a Messiah or Redeemer, who would set up an earthly kingdom and free Israel from the dominance of alien rulers, or the bondage of captivity which had beset them since the days of Abraham. This hope was very strong as the Caesars conquered most of the nearby world. Daniel, the prophet, had predicted that a descendant of the house of David would come to establish the Kingdom of Heaven on earth. The Israelites took hope in what the prophet Isaiah had said:

> When the enemy shall come in like a flood . . . the Redeemer shall come to Zion.*

* Isaiah 59:19,20

Just before Jesus' birth these prophesies were constantly discussed. Astrologers tried to compute the exact time of the Messiah's coming. There was to be the conjunction of several large planets, shining with the brilliance of one star. Wise men set out to reach Palestine at the exact time of this conjunction. They stopped to ask King Herod where the Messiah was to be born. Knowing the talk among the Israelites of the coming of their Redeemer and a new kingdom, Herod asked the wise men to let him know where they found the child. But those sages were too wise to report to the jealous, cruel ruler after they found the holy child.

For nearly two thousand years the Christian world has celebrated the birth of Jesus, which is said to have taken place in a stable in Bethlehem. It is a far more significant event than is indicated by singing angels, kneeling wise men, and a shining star. The lowly stable-cradle of Jesus' birth symbolizes the birth of the Christ spirit in the lowliest human being. Also the other high points of Jesus' life symbolize the various steps every human must take on his path from spiritual infancy to the ultimate of Christhood or union with God, when each of us may say, "I and my Father are One."

The four gospels according to St. Matthew, St. Mark, St. Luke, and St. John, written many years after Jesus lived, give varying accounts about the ancestral background of Jesus. St. Mark's Gospel, written 70 years after the time of Jesus, traces the ancestry through his father, Joseph, back to David, as the prophets had foretold. St. Matthew, a gospel written later, also traces the ancestry back from Joseph, though through a different line. Only St. Luke's Gospel gives the account of the Virgin birth. The Immaculate Conception is generally believed in by Roman Catholics, Eastern Orthodox Catholics, and many Protestants, while others interpret this concept symbolically in a cosmic and mystical sense as the birth of spirit in matter and a spiritual birth in each human being as he climbs the pathway from spiritual infancy, until he is the perfected man, a Christ. The different ideas on how to interpret the various scriptures of the Bible have led to much conflict and even bloodshed, and the separation of Christianity into many sects and denominations.

Though Jesus is said to have been born in Bethlehem of

Judea, where Joseph and Mary had gone for a tax census, he spent his childhood in Nazareth, where he helped in his father's carpenter shop. In his home of white stones, cut from the nearby mountains, his gentle mother Mary taught him the Mosaic laws. Some claim she was a member of the Essene group, whose headquarters were at Engaddi in Palestine, near the Dead Sea, where it is said she may have learned the deeper meaning of the Jewish scriptures. This tradition seems to be a plausible one. There was also a group of Essenes in Egypt on Lake Maoris. This could have been the destination of Joseph and Mary, who fled to Egypt with the holy child when Herod ordered all male Jews under two to be slain, so he could be certain this new Messiah did not grow up to oust him from his throne.

The exact date of Jesus' birth is unknown. Researchers differ among themselves. Some say it was about 4 B.C. However, the date of December 25th was arbitrarily set. Others maintain it was probably a century earlier. This latter period is given by Dr. Annie Besant, a profound student of the inner meanings of all religions, in her *Esoteric Christianity:*

"The child whose Jewish name has been turned into that of Jesus was born in Palestine, B.C. 105, during the consulate of Publius Rutilius Rufus and Gnaeus Mallius Maximum. His parents were well born though poor, and he was educated in a knowledge of the Hebrew scriptures. His fervent devotion and his gravity beyond his years led his parents to dedicate him to the religious and ascetic life, and soon after a visit to Jerusalem, in which the extraordinary intelligence and eagerness for knowledge of the youth were shown in his seeking the doctors of the Temple, he was sent to be trained in the Essene community in the southern Judean desert. When he had reached the age of nineteen he went on to the Essene monastery near Mount Serbal, a monastery which was much visited by learned men traveling from Persia and India to Egypt. . . . From this seat of mystic learning, he proceeded later to Egypt . . . and there the young Hebrew received the solemn consecration which prepared him for the Royal Priesthood he was later to attain."

The four gospels say nothing of the life of Jesus between the age of twelve, when he amazed the rabbis in the temple, and his thirtieth year when he began his ministry. Some authorities claim he taught in the Essene community before beginning his actual ministry to the people of Palestine.

Baptism and Temptation

After the scene in the Temple when Jesus was twelve, the next events reported in the Gospels took place when he was about thirty and appeared in the throng on the banks of the Jordan. John the Baptist, the bearded prophet, was denouncing Roman rule and trying to arouse the Israelites out of their apathy by proclaiming the imminent coming of the Redeemer who would save Israel. According to the Gospel record John glanced up, saw Jesus and said:

> There cometh one mightier than I after me, the latchet of whose shoes I am not worthy to stoop down and unloose.*

Then Jesus asked to be baptised by John, though the prophet said *he* should be baptised by Jesus. Baptism by immersion was an ancient custom, a symbol of washing away sins. It had been practiced for many centuries by the Hindus in the Ganga and by other religious groups.

Following his baptism, Jesus went into the wilderness to meditate on his coming work. Some researchers say this wilderness retreat was a cliff cavern overlooking the Dead Sea and the vineyards in the valley. According to the Gospels, he fasted for forty days and was tempted by the Devil with offers of worldly kingdoms and power.

Having resisted all temptations, Jesus at last left the retreat, knowing the kingdom he would preach about must be a spiritual one. On learning that John the Baptist had been imprisoned for trying to incite rebellion against Roman rule, Jesus knew the time had come to begin his efforts to save the Hebrew people.

Ministry of Jesus

Jesus chose his first disciples from among the fishermen by the Sea of Galilee. The first two were brothers, Peter and Andrew. Next he chose two other brothers, James and John. John was to become very close to Jesus in his understanding of the true mission

* Mark 1:7

of the Master. Eventually there were twelve disciples who went about with him, seeking to reform the malpractices into which Judaism had fallen.

Jesus taught in the synagogues, but more often in the open, where crowds gathered by the Sea of Galilee, the River Jordan, or on the verdant hillsides. People came from long distances to hear this new gospel. Its main themes were the love of God and the brotherhood of man. He tried to make his hearers understand that obeying the letter of the old Mosaic laws was not enough, that their actions must be motivated by love. Moses had brought them the law, now Jesus had come to proclaim the gospel of love. Both teachings were necessary if they were to attain the Christ-consciousness or the Kingdom of Heaven.

The radiating love of the teacher was so magnetic that he drew many to him. Struggling souls with blighted pasts found in him a sympathetic friend who did not condemn, but offered understanding and forgiveness.

Jesus was a man of strong feelings and emotions, who could show his righteous indignation when provoked too far. He drove avaricious merchants out of the synagogue on finding them haggling over the price of living creatures to be used for blood sacrifices. Such outbursts against existing malpractices provoked the Sadducees and Pharisees against him, for they had added many new laws to the original Mosaic commandments.

Some researchers maintain that Jesus learned the healing art during his years of training among the Essenes. The many cures brought about during his ministry must have been performed by the operation of spiritual forces, which can be manipulated only by a great soul dedicated to the ideal of love and service to humanity. The four gospels record that he made the lame walk, the blind see, and brought new life to those who were sick of soul. People came to him from long distances and from many strata of society to be healed of body and soul.

The Sermon on the Mount

Once when a great multitude had gathered, Jesus took them to a mountain (which symbolically means spiritual heights) and there preached his greatest sermon. This was no negative gospel, or condemnation of people who had strayed from the upward path. It dealt with inspiring truths and the teaching of the virtues, which lead to Christhood.

> Blessed are the pure in heart: for they shall see God.
> Blessed are the peacemakers: for they shall be called the children of God.[1]

Another statement which must have been of great comfort to his followers among the often-persecuted Jews was:

> Blessed are ye, when men shall revile you, and persecute you, and shall say all manner of evil against you falsely, for my sake.
> Rejoice, and be exceeding glad; for great is your reward in heaven.[2]

Instead of constantly condemning people for their mistakes, he kept reminding them of their potential goodness, affirming that they were sons of God and that it had not yet been revealed what they might become. In the Sermon on the Mount he said:

> Ye are the salt of the earth. . . . Ye are the light of the world.[3]

Another statement that must have eased the growing concern of the Jewish people about this new teacher was:

> Think not that I am come to destroy the law, or the prophets; I am not come to destroy, but to fulfil.[4]

During the long sermon, he gave them a simple, but profound prayer, which is still used daily by millions of Christians:

> Our Father, which art in heaven, Hallowed be thy name.
> Thy kingdom come. Thy will be done in earth, as it is in heaven.
> Give us this day our daily bread.
> And forgive us our debts, as we forgive our debtors.
> And lead us not into temptation, but deliver us from evil: For thine is the kingdom, and the power, and the glory, forever, Amen.[5]

When Jesus came down from the mountain, he continued to teach and heal lepers, the lame, the blind, and those sick from evil doing. He spoke most often to the simple people through

[1] Matthew 5:8,9
[2] Matthew 5:11,12
[3] Matthew 5:13,14
[4] Matthew 5:17
[5] Matthew 6:9-13

stories and parables in the language they could understand. He spoke of teachers being fishers of men and of stilling one's untamed emotions by the power of God within.

To his disciples, however, he explained the inner meanings of his teachings, for most of them were spiritually evolved men. He said to them:

> Unto you it is given to know the mystery of the kingdom of God: but to those that are without, all these things are done in parables.[1]

Jesus' message was ahead of his time. He could not make the foreign powers controlling the country, nor the majority of the Jews, understand that he was preaching of a spiritual kingdom instead of an earthly one. He was bold in his condemnation of some of the religious malpractices of the day. He rebuked their observance of the letter of the law rather than the spirit. The Pharisees condemned him for breaking the Sabbath when he let his disciples gather grain in the fields and eat it. The rabbis were jealous of his power to heal the sick and of his great popularity. They accused him of witchcraft in healing a mentally ill man. He replied that if he were the Devil he would not cast himself out of another man. The people in general began to turn against him in disappointment when they found he was not restoring the earthly kingdom of Israel.

The Transfiguration

Finally the bitterness and jealousy became so great that the lives of Jesus and his disciples were in jeopardy and so they fled to Caesarea. The saddened Jesus felt his mission and work had failed. Knowing that his was to be the inevitable fate of a martyr, he nevertheless journeyed toward Jerusalem. From a height overlooking the holy city he said in anguish:

> O Jerusalem, Jerusalem, which killest the prophets, and stonest them that are sent unto thee; how often would I have gathered thy children together, as a hen doth gather her brood under her wings, and ye would not! [2]

This was a poignant moment in Jesus' life, for it is a great sorrow to be rejected by those who need help and will not accept it.

[1] Mark: 4,11
[2] Luke 13:34

Knowing the time for his martyrdom was near, Jesus wanted to get away from the crowd and pray for strength for the ordeal to come. Generally he had gone alone for this renewal of the spirit, but this time he took his most beloved disciples, Peter, James, and John with him to the mountain top. There the disciples saw him enveloped in a blinding light, his face and garments shining like the sun. With him appeared Moses and Elias and the disciples heard a voice saying:

> This is my beloved Son, in whom I am well pleased; hear ye him.[1]

The Master Jesus had long since known the birth of the divine spirit within himself. He had submitted to John's baptism as a symbol of cleansing from past broken laws. This was followed by the temptation in the wilderness, when he chose between an earthly kingdom and a spiritual one. Then at the transfiguration, the personal self merged into the Christ-consciousness when he was called "Son of God," a peak to be reached by each human soul on his path through many lives from animal-man to divine-man.

Rebirth

As Jesus and the three came down from the heights, the disciples asked him about Elias, who had appeared with him. They had understood from the prophecies that Elias was to come before the Messiah, when the kingdom of Israel was to be restored. Jesus answered them and said:

> But I say unto you, That Elias is come already, and they knew him not, but have done unto him whatsoever they listed. Likewise shall also the Son of man suffer of them.
> Then the disciples understood that he spake unto them of John the Baptist.[2]

There are other evidences that Jesus talked to his disciples of rebirth when they asked him concerning a blind man he had healed:

> Master, who did sin, this man, or his parents, that he was born blind?

[1] Matthew 17:5
[2] Matthew 17:12,13

Church of All Nations, Garden of Gethsemane, Jerusalem.

Jesus answered, Neither this man sinned, nor his parents: but that the works of God should be made manifest in him.[1]

Also Jesus promised to come again when he said:

I will come again, and receive you unto myself.[2]

In the mystical Book of Revelation John wrote of the triumphal consummation of the soul's long struggle through many lives up many paths toward perfection:

Him that overcometh will I make a pillar in the temple of my God, and he shall go no more out.[3]

The laws of rebirth were evidently not understood by the less educated people of Palestine though many church Fathers wrote of it. The Sadducees did not even believe in life after death, so the idea that a soul must pass through many physical incarnations before reaching perfection was unacceptable to them. But in his great wisdom Jesus knew how to teach people according to the needs and stage of their development. To the disciples he could talk face to face.

Crucifixion and Resurrection

From the Mount of Transfiguration Jesus went down to continue his teaching and healing. Great throngs now followed to glorify his name as he went in a triumph of praise toward Jerusalem for the Feast of the Passover, prepared for him and his disciples in an upper chamber. There he instituted the Lord's Supper or the Eucharist which is celebrated today in all Christian churches.

By that time the fickle mobs had turned against him, urged on by jealous rabbis and Roman authorities, who were afraid of his growing influence over the people. Knowing that he was to be betrayed by one of his disciples and crucified, Jesus went into the Garden of Gethsemane to pray and make contact with God to draw strength from the Infinite for the coming ordeal. It was his disciple Judas who betrayed him to the Romans. He was tried in the Roman court before Pilate and condemned to be crucified. The betrayal by Judas is symbolic of the betrayal made by the weaker aspects of each soul facing life's crucifixions. But Jesus

[1] John 9:2,3
[2] John 14:3
[3] Revelation 3:12

was strong enough to endure the cross of agony and in the end to say, "It is finished." He had endured all life's gruelling tests, had learned to conform to all God's laws, and to feel compassion and love even for those who were crucifying him, when he exclaimed "They know not what they do." He had now become a pillar in the temple of God and need not go out any more.

So great was the love of this Christed Jesus for the humanity he longed to help that three days after the Crucifixion he appeared to those closest to him in his subtle body. Years later Paul, his disciple, explained that there were "celestial bodies and bodies terrestrial." * Jesus' appearance assured his disciples and all mankind that the soul continues to exist after the physical body ceases to function. The crucifixion and resurrection of Jesus became the foundation on which the Christian church built much of its doctrine.

Jesus continued to appear to his disciples and to teach them at intervals for some time after the crucifixion. Now he hoped to make them understand that his was a spiritual kingdom, not an earthly one, and that they must go into all the world to spread his message. Some researchers say he continued to teach them for forty days, others claim that he kept up occasional contacts for about fifty years.

Birth of the Church

Stories of Jesus' teachings and healings spread widely, though nothing was written down for many years. No doubt the story of the feeding of the five thousand with a few loaves and fishes whose symbolic meaning was interpreted literally, was being repeated for several generations before being written in the gospels. To those who understood the inner meaning of what Jesus taught, the first miracle of turning water into wine at the wedding feast meant that water, representing the emotional nature, could be transmuted into wine, or spiritual faculties. It was 70 A.D. before these accounts were finally written down in the first Gospel of St. Mark.

The leaders of the Christian movement organized themselves into communities, where all possessions were owned in common. The earliest of these communities were composed of Jewish people. They called each other "Brother" or "Sister," looked after the sick, and shared what they had with each other. When the

* Corinthians 15:40

rabbis arrested some of them, the organization became more secret. After the Romans destroyed Solomon's Temple in 70 A.D., the Jews were driven out of their holy city. The new Christian sect was then scattered and carried the new religion into other countries.

Saint Paul

Among the Jews who persecuted the Christians was a rabbi and tentmaker named Saul of Tarsus. He had been educated in Jerusalem under Rabbi Gamaliel. He had no patience with this new religion, for he considered Jesus a fanatic. The high council, under which he preached, asked him to help suppress the Christian movement. However, on the road to Damascus, where he was going to take action against the followers of Jesus, he was suddenly enveloped in a glow of blinding light and heard Jesus ask, "Saul, Saul, why persecutest thou me?" * So great was the experience that for three days Saul could neither see nor eat. A follower of Jesus, Ananias, healed him by explaining the true meaning of the message of Christ. Saul, realizing the teachings were divinely inspired, was converted. After that his name was changed to Paul.

He astonished the Jewish people by beginning to preach the Christian message in the synagogues. Later he traveled to Asia Minor and Europe, becoming the first Christian missionary and the founder of the Christian Church. The teachings finally gained more converts among the Gentiles than among the Jews. Both the Greeks and Romans were ready for a new religion. So many minor gods had emerged around their chief gods, Zeus and Jupiter, that the people had little reverence for any of them.

Groups and churches were formed in Syria, Macedonia, Crete, Athens, Corinth, Rome, and many other places. The converts met for preaching and praying on Sundays, the day on which, according to tradition, Jesus had risen from the dead. On Wednesdays and Fridays they fasted and met to pray. Between visits to his congregations Paul wrote many letters to the new groups, explaining the meanings of Christ's teachings and encouraging those who were being persecuted for their beliefs. These letters were preserved and eventually became part of the

* Acts 9:4

New Testament.

Paul understood the real meaning of Christ's teachings even better than some who had known him personally and had been his disciples. He understood that Jesus, the man, had attained Christhood, which is a possibility for every human soul. He used the word *Christ,* not as the name of a person, but as the goal of human attainment, for by following the teachings one may attain this perfection, Christhood. Paul said:

> My little children, of whom I travail in birth again until Christ be formed in you.[1]

He constantly reminded his converts that they must struggle against the cravings of the flesh and the world and work toward perfecting themselves:

> Till we all come in the unity of the faith, and of the knowledge of the Son of God, unto a perfect man, unto the measure of the stature of the fullness of Christ.[2]

Again he spoke of "the Christ in you, the hope of glory."

He taught the brotherhood of all humanity by saying that the divine spark, or Christ, dwelt in all men:

> Where there is neither Greek nor Jew, circumcision nor uncircumcision, Barbarian, Scythian, bond nor free: but Christ is all and in all.[3]

Early in his ministry Paul's followers were called Christians for the first time. But like Jesus, Paul also was destined for martyrdom. After twice being held a prisoner in Rome, he was finally executed by the cruel Nero.

Until the third century, Christians were persecuted by the Roman emperors, so their meetings had to be held in secret, and many died as martyrs for their faith. When Emperor Constantine was converted to Christianity in 312 A.D., Christianity became the religion of the Roman Empire and spread rapidly. Tragically, as the new religion came under the dominance of the Empire, persecutions increased against those who refused to accept it; and, within the faith, martyrdom was meted out to others who deviated from the dogma created by the empire church. More

[1] Galatians 4:19
[2] Ephesians 4:13
[3] Col. 3:11

blood has been shed due to intolerance among so-called Christians than in any other faith.

Christian Scriptures

Research shows that the Epistles of St. Paul, included in the New Testament, were written about 50 A.D. The earliest of these letters was the First Epistle to the Thessalonians. This was followed by a series of letters to the various groups which Paul had established in Asia Minor and Europe. All were written in Greek.

About 100 A.D., when the New Testament was first compiled, Paul's letters were preceded by the four gospels, which give varying accounts of Jesus' life. St. Mark was written in 70 A.D. and was followed by the other three gospels, those according to St. Matthew, St. Luke, and St. John.

Letters to the early churches were written also by Peter, James, John, and others. Finally there is John's mystical book of the Revelation, which must be understood in its inner, symbolical meaning. All this writing was done within a period of one hundred years after the time of Jesus.

Some of these books were translated from the original Hebrew to Greek and then to Latin. It was not until about the fourth century, after the Roman church was established that decisions were finally made concerning which books would be included in the New Testament.

The New Testament now has many versions, having been translated into different languages for numerous sects with varying interpretations. The New Testament used by the Roman Catholic Church and the King James and Revised translations, used by Protestant Christians, vary slightly. The Bible, including the Old and New Testaments, is the most widely distributed book in the world. It sells millions of copies every year in 195 different complete translations, and may be found in practically every city in the world.

Christian Sacraments

Many Protestant Christians observe only two great sacraments: baptism and communion. Roman and Eastern Orthodox Catholics, and Episcopalians, among the Protestants, and a few smaller sects celebrate seven sacraments: baptism, confirmation, communion, unction, penance, marriage, and ordination.

Baptism is a rite almost universally observed among many of the great religions of the world. It symbolizes the washing away of stains, or one's broken laws, or one's sins, as the Christians call this. For many centuries the Hindus have bathed in the Ganga as a ritual of spiritual purification. It is also a sacred rite among other non-Christian people. In Roman Catholic and some Protestant churches baptism consists of sprinkling water that has been blessed on the head of the convert. In Baptist Protestant Churches and a few others, baptism is by immersion, as Jesus went into the Jordan and was immersed by John the Baptist. Catholics and some Protestants practice infant baptism, as a dedication of the child to the church of Christ. In other churches members are baptised when they have reached sufficient understanding to promise to live the Christian life. In some churches the applicant undergoes a period of instruction, preceding baptism and church membership. Other churches accept membership merely on a profession of faith in the teachings of Jesus Christ.

Communion, or the Eucharist, is universally observed with slight variations in all Christian churches in memory of the last supper which Jesus had with his disciples just before his crucifixion. St. Luke reported what Jesus said in that upper chamber during the Passover Supper:

> And he took bread and gave thanks, and brake it and gave unto them saying, This is my body given for you; this do in remembrance of me.
> Likewise also the cup after supper, saying, This cup is the new testament in my blood, which is shed for you.[1]

Practically all Christians use a ritual for marriage. Dr. Annie Besant explained the symbolical meaning of this ceremony: "The Sacrament of Marriage shows out the marks of a sacrament as clearly and as definitely as do Baptism and the Eucharist. Both the outer and the inner grace are there. The material is the Ring — the circle which is the symbol of the everlasting. The Word of Power is the ancient formula, 'In the name of the Father and of the Son, and of the Holy Ghost.' The sign of Power is the joining of hands, symbolizing the joining of the lives. These make up the outer essentials of the Sacrament." [2]

[1] Luke 22:19,20
[2] *Esoteric Christianity*, by Annie Besant

Christians of all faiths join in Easter sunrise service at Hollywood Bowl, California.   Photograph by A. Devaney, Inc., N. Y.

Christian Holy Days

The most universally celebrated holy days of the Christians are Christmas, the day chosen to celebrate the birth of Jesus, and Easter Sunday, which celebrates the resurrection. There are no historical records of the actual dates of these events. The times chosen are periods in which many other religions also hold religious festivals, connected with the winter solstice and the spring equinox. Over a hundred different dates have been used by various Christian sects in celebrating the birth of Jesus.

The matter was finally settled by Pope Julius I, in 337 A.D. and St. Chrysostom, writing in 390, says: "On this day (i.e., 25th December) also the birth of Christ was lately fixed at Rome, in order that while the heathen were busy with their ceremonies (the Brumalia, in honour of Baccus) the Christians might perform their rites undisturbed." *

For many ages this season had been used to celebrate the birth of religious teachers; among them the Egyptian Horus and the Persian Mithras. In most of these ancient religions the holy child came as a savior of men, and the mother was called a virgin.

In Christian countries and among scattered missions, Christmas is celebrated in many ways. Germany began the custom of having candle-lighted trees, laden with gifts, a practice which is now generally followed. Other customs vary. Dutch children leave their wooden shoes for the gifts of St. Nicholas, the spirit of Christmas, while American children hang their stockings by the mantel. Churches are made festive with Christmas greens and lighted candles, while Christmas carols fill the air and crowds gather to hear over again the glorious music of Handel's *Messiah*. In spite of so many outward forms and the commercialized aspects of Christmas, throngs gather in churches in gratitude for the birth of the Christ child.

Though Christmas now has a fixed date, the celebration of Easter, or the resurrection is governed by the position of the sun and moon after the spring equinox, so that Easter is the first Sunday following the first full moon after the spring equinox.

As in other lands and among other religions this spring celebration is a time of renewal. New clothes, blooming flowers, and inspiring music are the outer symbols of this season of gratitude

* *Esoteric Christianity,* by Annie Besant

and hope that as the soul of Jesus survived the death of the physical body, so shall we all go on to more glorious living in this promise of eternal life.

Christianity Spreads

For several centuries Christianity had its center in Rome under a succession of Popes, who gradually gained more power over the lives, beliefs, and religious practices of the Christian world. Finally in the fifteenth and sixteenth centuries, the Protestant Reformation began when Martin Luther and John Calvin rebelled against the authority of the Popes and some of the doctrines taught by the Roman Catholic Church. This eventually led to the formation of many different sects or denominations in Protestant Christianity; Lutherans, Presbyterians, Methodists, Baptists, and many others, each with its own interpretation of the Old and New Testaments.

Today there are approximately 275 million Roman Catholics, scattered throughout the world, 221 million Protestants, and 124 million Eastern Orthodox Catholics.

Many thousands of books have been written, explaining the New Testament. Some of the world's greatest orators have preached the Christian gospel. It has challenged the best creative efforts of sculptors and architects in building churches and temples such as St. Peter's in Rome, the Cathedral of Notre Dame in Paris, and the Cathedral of St. John the Divine in New York. Poets, musicians, dramatists, and novelists have been inspired to present the Christian truth in varying forms. Through the simple music of "Silent Night, Holy Night" and the exalting "Halleluiah Chorus" of Handel's *Messiah* its message has given inspiration to Christian hearts all over the world.

Suggested Further Reading:

Bible (King James Version, New English Bible, and other revised versions).

ALLEGRO, JOHN
The Dead Sea Scrolls, A Reappraisal, Penguin Books, Inc., Baltimore, Maryland, 1964 (A Pelican paperback).

BESANT, ANNIE
Esoteric Christianity, The Theosophical Publishing House, Wheaton, Illinois, 1970 (Quest Book paperback).

Seven Great Religions, The Theosophical Publishing House, Adyar, Madras, India, 1966.

GAER, JOSEPH
Love of the New Testament, Grosset & Dunlap, Inc., New York.

Love of the Old Testament, Grosset & Dunlap, Inc., New York

GROVE, DAISY E.
Mystery Teaching of the Bible, The Theosophical Publishing House, London, 1962.

HALL, MANLY P.
How to Understand Your Bible (Old and New Testaments), Philosophical Research Society, Los Angeles, 1942.

HODSON, GEOFFREY
The Hidden Wisdom in the Holy Bible, Vols. 1 & 2, The Theosophical Publishing House, Wheaton, Illinois, 1967 and 1969 (Quest Book paperbacks).

HUELIN, DR. GORDON (Ed.)
All in Good Faith, An Anthology of Western Christianity, Leslie Frewin, London, 1966.

KINGSLAND, WILLIAM
Gnosis or Ancient Wisdom in the Christian Scriptures, The Theosophical Publishing House, Wheaton, Illinois, 1970 (Quest Book paperback).

LIFE EDITORIAL STAFF
The World's Great Religions, Golden Press, New York, 1967.

SCHURE, EDOUARD
Jesus the Last Great Initiate, Rider & Co., London, 1923.

MORTON, H. V.
In the Steps of the Master, Dodd, Mead & Co., New York, 1934.

TRANTER, GERALD
Mystery Teachings and Christianity, The Theosophical Publishing House, Wheaton, Illinois, 1969 (Quest Book paperback).

WASSIL, ALY
The Wisdom of Christ, Harper & Row, New York, 1965.

WEATHERHEAD, LESLIE D.
The Christian Agnostic, Abingdon Press, Nashville, Tenn., 1965.

Minaret of great Badshahi Mosque, Lahore, Pakistan. Built in 1674, it is the largest mosque in the world.

Chapter VII

The Path of Islam

Early Arabs

When Abraham banished Hagar and his eldest son, Ishmael, into the desert, he created a cause whose effects have stretched over thousands of years, affecting millions of people.

After her exile, Hagar, fearing death from thirst and starvation, wandered with her son toward Egypt. In his anger and frustration, young Ishmael kicked the sands of the desert and a spring of water gushed forth. Other traditions claim an angel appeared at Hagar's prayer for help and led them to a spring.

Hagar and her son lived beside the spring. Other desert people settled near the miraculous waters, which they named Zem Zem. Eventually Ishmael married an Egyptian woman, and they had twelve sons. Their many descendants grew into clans and then tribes, spreading over the Arabian desert.

During that early history, a black meteorite fell near the spring. The Ishmaelites thought it was heaven-sent. Some traditions claim that Abraham heard of the meteorite, which they called the Black Stone. He came to help his son build a simple square stone structure around it, which they called the Kaaba, or Ka'ba. The city that grew up around this shrine was called Mecca. It later became the sacred city of the Muslim or Islamic faith.

When the Black Stone fell, Ishmael is said to have heard a voice from heaven promising that his descendants would become more powerful than those of his half-brother, Isaac. This ancient prediction seems to have come true, for today there are 466 million followers of the prophet Mohammed, a descendant of Ishmael, and about 13 million Jews, descendants of Isaac.

In those early centuries, the Arabs became a very war-like people. Tribes squabbled with one another, fought over oases in the desert and over trade. They spread west to the Mediterranean, east to the Persian Gulf and occupied the lower Arabian peninsula. Mecca became the center to which they all came for trade, to drink at the sacred spring, and kiss the Black Stone in the Kaaba. The city was on the spice and trade route between India and Syria, so the Arabs had contacts with other races and beliefs. The camel-riding traders were Hindus, Jews, and Christians.

Mohammed

In the sixth century A.D. the keeper of the Kaaba was Abdul Muttalib, a member of the ruling Quarish clan. Abdul's son died just before his wife gave birth to a son, Mohammed, in 570 A.D. This son was destined to become the founder of the Muslim religion, correctly called Islam. Mystical traditions are connected with his birth as they are with the births of other religious founders. Jesus' birth was heralded by prophets, a brilliant star, and singing angels. Gautama Buddha was said to have spoken immediately after birth, announcing the completion of the cycle of his physical births. On Mohammed's arrival on the physical plane, it was reported that he opened his eyes and said, *"La ilaha Allah, Mohammed rasul Allahi."* (There is no God but Allah, and Mohammed is the prophet of Allah.)

The boy grew up in the religious atmosphere of the Kaaba, where his grandfather was caretaker. After his mother died when he was seven, he lived with an uncle and became a shepherd. Like Abraham, his ancestor, Mohammed had time in the quiet desert to meditate on the mysteries of creation and the Creator. Early in life he was distressed by the degraded lives of so many of his peo-

96

ple. Once more, as it had been since the beginning of humanity, a teacher was needed to help. Just as the Buddha had come to India in her time of need, Confucius had rescued China, and Jesus had come to proclaim the gospel of love for all people, so Mohammed came to the Arabs to proclaim strict laws to train an undisciplined people, to rescue them from idol worship with the religion of one God.

By the sixth century A.D., the Arabs had become an illiterate, superstitious, and warlike people. Some were nature-worshipers, regarding mountains, trees, springs, and rocks as sacred. Most had forgotten the one God of their ancestors, Abraham and Ishmael. They placed idols all around the city of Mecca and near the Kaaba. The mercenaries in the holy city began to charge for the spring water that many pilgrims came to drink. Greed, drunkenness, gambling, and lust dominated the people.

Mohammed brooded over these tragic conditions. When he was older he led camel caravans across the desert to trade in Egypt and Syria. In Syria he learned from Jews and Christians about their one God. Though he was illiterate, he listened to the recitals of their sacred scriptures.

When Mohammed was twenty-four, he married the wealthy widow, Khadija, who had employed him to lead her trade caravans. She was over forty and had several children. He lived happily with her for twenty-six years, during which time he rose to the religious leadership of the Arab people.

Mohammed was a short stocky man with coal black, curly hair and beard. He had great strength and physical endurance. During a terrible desert storm the sacred Black Stone was dislodged from its niche in the Kaaba. Mohammed's great strength enabled him to replace it. This won him much favor with the superstitious and impressionable people.

The Teachings

For about fifteen years after his marriage, Mohammed struggled within his own soul for a way to save the Arabs from their degradation. Every year in the month of Ramadan, he went alone to a cave on Mount Hira to meditate. When he was about forty, as he lay on the desert sands, he went into a trance and heard the Archangel Gabriel speaking to him.

"Read," the angel said. Mohammed tried to explain that he could not read. Then light shone all around him and he found he could read from a tablet that the angel held:

Oh, thou who art wrapped, rise up and warn!
And the Lord magnify,
And thy raiment glorify,
And abomination shun,
And grant not favors to gain increase!
And wait for the Lord.

Then the angel gave Mohammed instructions about the creation, about man and the angels, and showed him something of what lay ahead of him. Finally the Archangel Gabriel said, "Rise, thou art the Prophet of God; go forth and cry in the name of the Lord."

Thus Mohammed had his first message which was later included in the Koran, the sacred scripture of the Muslims. On his return home Mohammed told his wife, Khadija, of his experience and his orders to teach the people. She encouraged him to follow the search for truth, so Mohammed continued going to his retreat in the cave of Mount Hira, where more instructions were given him on how to help his people.

In addition to his wife, Mohammed slowly gained other disciples, a young relative named Ali, and Abu Bakr. Three years later he had only thirty disciples. They went with him to his retreat to write down what the prophet repeated as Gabriel continued to give him instructions. These sayings were recorded on palm leaves, bits of leather, sun-bleached bones, or anything that was convenient when the prophet was receiving instructions.

As Mohammed's followers increased, so did opposition to his teachings. The Arabs fought fiercely to maintain their dissolute way of life. To do away with drunkenness would destroy the profit in their vineyards. Fighting their rivals had become a way of life, while greed and cheating were part of their trade. They were ready to fight any who would make changes. They scorned the teacher who claimed he had instructions from Heaven.

Mohammed had begun his first sermon by saying, "There is no God but Allah, and Mohammed is the prophet of Allah." His followers became known as Muslims, or Moslems, and the religion was given the name Islam, which means submission, for every

Muslim must submit to the discipline and laws laid down in the Koran.

One day some pilgrims from Yathrib (later called Medina) came to hear Mohammed preach. They asked what his teachings were and Mohammed explained briefly:

Allah is the one God, and Mohammed is his Prophet.
Give up idolatry,
Do not steal,
Do not kill,
Do not slander,
And never become intoxicated,
If you follow these teachings you follow Islam.

Among these were four of the old Mosaic commandments, expressed in different language, with one important addition — abstinence from intoxicating liquors — which was a crying need of the Arabs at that time.

Hijra

People from Medina came often to hear Mohammed, and eventually he had many converts among them. The people of Mecca, especially his own Quarish clan, opposed his teachings and eventually plotted to kill him. With his faithful disciple, Abu Bakr, Mohammed fled on his camel, Al Kaswa. Angry mobs tried to overtake him, but Mohammed and Abu Bakr hid in a cave for three days and finally reached Medina about seven days later, on Friday, the twelfth of Rabi-el-Awwal in 622 A.D. This migration is now known in the Muslim world as Hijra (the flight). The people of Medina believed Mohammed was the promised messenger, and this period is considered the beginning of his ministry.

When believers from Mecca followed their teacher, a real brotherhood with the people of Medina was established to help spread the new religion. Medina was a walled city, so Mohammed organized an army for defense against their enemies. He established the Islamic state and for eight years continued to live in Medina, teaching many people. He won many battles against the enemies of his reformation.

However Mecca was still considered a sacred city, for the ancient Kaaba was there with the holy spring and the Black Stone in the shrine. Treaties were made with the people in Mecca but these were broken. Mohammed raised an army of 12,000 Muslims and marched against Mecca, praying for a bloodless battle. His prayer was answered, for the people of Mecca fled at the approach of the great army. Mohammed marched in and his men destroyed all the idols, including the most important one, Habel, near the Kaaba.

Mohammed forgave his enemies and eventually most of them returned to the city to embrace his new religion. Within two more years most of the Arabs had become his followers. All during his ministry the Prophet spoke out for tolerance of other religions, explaining that the Arabs had a common ancestor with Jews and Christians and that all believed in one God.

Mohammed did all he could to save the Arabs from their degradation. Before his death in 632 A.D., he had given them a better code of living and established the Islamic religion that was eventually to spread over Asia, Africa, and Europe. The essence of the Islamic religion may be summed up as follows:

The Koran teaches belief in one God and the brotherhood of man. It states that no intermediary is needed between God and man. The believers are encouraged to gain a knowledge of the universe and of themselves and to use nature's forces for the benefit of humanity. Both extreme materialism and extreme asceticism are condemned, for man is warned to seek the middle way. (This also the Buddha had taught long ago in India.) Man's happiness or misery, whether in this life or the next, depends entirely on his own actions, and God accepts no intercession on behalf of another. The Koran advocates the establishment of a united Arab kingdom for the benefit of the Muslims and the whole world. Muslims were told to work for religious tolerance and peace among all nations. By these definite instructions Muslims were given directions for a better life.

The Caliphs

After Mohammed's death, his faithful disciple, Abu Bakr, became head of the Islamic faith, and was called Caliph. He also became ruler throughout the Islamic kingdom. He was followed by Omar, Osman, and Ali. Ali had accepted Mohammed's teachings when a youth and eventually married Mohammed's daughter, Fatima. The Muslims argued over who would succeed Mohammed as Caliph, and split into two sections. The Sunnites wanted the Caliph chosen from among his disciples. The Shi'ites thought he should be descended from Mohammed's grandson, Hussain, who was the son of Fatima and Ali. From these two divisions of Islam many denominations developed.

During the reign of the elected Caliph, the Islamic faith spread into countries conquered by the Muslims. They marched into Persia, Iraq, Syria, Egypt, North Africa, Palestine, and parts of India and China, conquering and converting the people. After the death of Ali, the position of Caliph became hereditary.

The Koran

After Mohammed's death, Abu Bakr, Ali, and others began collecting the prophet's teachings. Many of his sermons had been memorized, others had been written down by his disciples on whatever material was available. The compilation began eighteen years after Mohammed's death. It took five years to select what would be included in the sacred scriptures. The result was the Qu'ran, or Koran, which contains 30 *Souvaks,* or chapters. The whole is about the length of the Christian New Testament. The Koran was originally written in Arabic. At first no translations were allowed, but today the Koran may be read in many languages, including Persian, English, and Turkish. However it is almost impossible to get the true meaning of the original Arabic scripture into another language, for a slight mistake in the translation of the vowels will give an inaccurate meaning.

This book gives minute details regulating the lives of the followers of Islam. Some of the Islamic customs and rituals are similar to the Jewish and Christian, for Mohammed had learned about those religions before formulating his own. Some of the verses of the Koran are prefaced by, "God has said," and are believed to be divinely inspired. Other passages begin with, "The Prophet said." The Muslims believe the Koran is a copy of a "Heavenly Book," which was given to Mohammed bit by bit over a period of 23 years.

In addition to the moral, ethical, and spiritual teachings, the Koran contains stories similar to those in the Old Testament. It presents slightly different accounts of the creation, the flood, Adam, Noah, Abraham, Joseph, Moses, the Prophets, and Jesus.

101

It agrees that these prophets were sent to various people, but that Mohammed was sent for the whole world, and is the universal prophet.

The Koran also contains laws of sanitation and health, similar to those established by Moses for the Israelites. There are many different interpretations of Islam, as there are of other religions. Orthodox Muslims believe that on the day of Judgment the followers of Mohammed, who have broken laws, will be punished accordingly, but will not go to Hell. Those who have abided by the teachings will go straight to Heaven, and those who do not believe in their prophet will be lost.

Islamic Beliefs and Rituals

One of the strict rules laid down in the Koran is for Muslims to pray five times a day, at dawn, noon, afternoon, sunset, and after sunset. Before performing these prayers ablutions must be made by bathing the face, forearms, hands, and even rinsing the mouth and nostrils. Every Muslim uses the prayer, which they call *Al-Fatiha:*

> In the name of God, the Beneficent, the Merciful,
> Praise be to God, the Cherisher and Sustainer of the
> Worlds, the Beneficent and Merciful
> Master of the Day of Judgment.
> Thee do we worship, and Thine aid do we seek,
> Show us the straight way,
> The way of those on whom Thou hast bestowed Thy grace,
> Those whose portion is not wrath and who go not astray.

This prayer is said in the native tongue of each follower of Islam, and their word for God is always Allah. A Muslim must prostrate himself when praying and face toward Mecca.

Every Muslim must fast during the ninth month of the Islamic year, which is called Ramadan. This was the month in which Mohammed was first given instructions by the Archangel Gabriel about his mission in the world. The Jews and Christians, with whom Mohammed had traded, had long been observing fast days, but the Islam fasting was a little different. They fasted only during the daylight hours, from dawn to dark. Today during the period of Ramadan the Muslims eat lightly, attend to what business is absolutely necessary, and spend as much time as possible in prayer and meditation.

Pilgrimage to Mecca. The Holy Mosque of Mecca is filled with hundreds of thousands of devout Muslims from all parts of the Islamic world. In the center is the Kaaba, the most sacred of Islamic shrines.

The Koran also required that every Muslim make a pilgrimage to Mecca at least once in his lifetime. This has been a great factor in binding the followers of Mohammed into a closely-knit religious group, making a brotherhood of many people of various ethnic strains. During the twelfth month of the Muslim year caravans of camels, donkeys, cars, and many on foot cross the desert to Mecca. No one except a follower of Islam may enter the sacred city, though a few under disguise have slipped in to report on what goes on.

On the pilgrimage men wear a seamless white robe and do not shave or cut their hair. They must maintain an attitude of brotherliness toward all living things and carefully avoid breaking any laws of the Koran during their pilgrimage.

On arrival in Mecca the pilgrim must run seven times around the Kaaba, stopping each time to kiss or touch the Black Stone. Then in imitation of Hagar's frantic search for water for herself and Ishmael, the Moslem runs seven times between the hills of Safa and Mawa. And before leaving he must stand in the desert sun from noon to sundown on the Mount of Mercy as Mohammed had stood in the presence of God. This is followed by three days of feasting; then before leaving, the pilgrim makes a farewell run around the Kaaba.

Today Mecca is a city of about 90,000 population and is the capital of Saudi Arabia. During the month of the pilgrimage the population more than doubles. The chief interest of the inhabitants is preparing for the coming of the pilgrims. This celebration has brought together many thousands, representing various races and customs, in a strong bond of brotherhood, under one God and one code of religious and ethical teachings.

Next to Mecca, Jerusalem was at one time Islam's most holy city. Caliph Omar conquered it in 650 A.D. On the ruins of Solomon's Temple, which the Romans had destroyed, Omar built a Muslim mosque.

Another celebration of the Muslims is the Hijra, in memory of Mohammed's flight from Mecca to Medina to begin the actual establishment of the Islamic faith. This is observed in the first month of the Islamic year. Each month begins at the time of the new moon, so the months alternate with 29 and 30 days each, making a year of 354 days.

The Sufis

As in all other religions, Islam has its mystical aspect, in which the profound, more devout student seeks the inner truths that are at the core of all truly spiritual teachings. During Mohammed's life, and for a time thereafter, those who had been closest to him understood the mystical aspects of his teachings. In the same way the close disciples of Gautama Buddha and Jesus Christ understood the profound spiritual truths, the inner meanings behind the laws, forms, and ceremonies.

As in the other great religions, after the teacher was gone, his followers began to find varying interpretations in the scriptures and eventually broke up into sects. One group which tried to preserve and understand the inner depths of Mohammed's teachings was the Sufis. They flourished in the eighth and ninth centuries, especially in Persia, where much mystical poetry was written.

The Sufis, like the mystical groups of all other religions, tried to explain the laws of rebirth. Sharf-ud-Din Maneri, a Sufi teacher, wrote:

> O Brother, know for certain that this work has been before thee and me in bygone ages, and that each man has already reached a certain age. No one has begun this work for the first time.[1]

Although rebirth is not an accepted tenet of Islam, Mohammed himself apparently believed that this truth gave the key to an understanding of life that was otherwise inexplicable. In the Koran the saying is repeated that "God generates beings and sends them back to earth over and over until they return permanently to Him." [2] There are also hints that some of the deeper students of Islam believed the personality to be only a mask worn for one life, and that those for whom they had affinity were old kindred, though they met in this life in new persons and under new names. In the New Koran we find an explanation of the personality of man:

> And when his body falleth off altogether, as an old fish-shell, his soul doeth well by the releasing, and formeth a new one instead. . . . Ye who now lament to go out of this body wept also when ye were born into it. . . . The person of man is only

[1] *Letters from a Sufi Teacher,* translated by Baijnath Singh
[2] Koran, XXX.10

105

a mask which the soul putteth on for a season; it weareth its proper time and then is cast off, and another is worn in its stead. . . . I tell you, of a truth, that the spirits which now have affinity shall be kindred together, although they all meet in new persons and names.[1]

Finding the masses unable to understand some of the more profound truths, the Sufis withdrew into monastaries, where they could meditate and write. Abd Allah al-Balyani, a 13th century Sufi, foresaw the miracle of the 20th Century when he wrote:

When the secret of the atom is clear, the secret of all created things, both external and internal is clear, and thou dost not see in this world or the next aught but God.[2]

As the centuries passed some Sufis began to use for selfish ends the powers they had gained through deeper study. A few became sorcerers, others snake charmers and drug addicts, so that the order fell into disrepute, but the profound knowledge revealed through the writings of the truly devout ones remains a monument to the original integrity of the order.

Faith in the Prophet Mohammed and his teachings has developed a strong and loyal people, who are not afraid to kneel in prayer wherever they are. As had the Jews and Christians before them, they helped spread the worship of one God and the Brotherhood of Man to the ends of the earth.

[1] *Reincarnation, an East-West Anthology,* Joseph Head and S. L. Cranston
[2] *Encyclopaedia Brittanica,* Sufism, Vol. 21

Suggested Further Reading:

Koran (Several Editions).

ALI, A. YUSAF
The Message of Islam, John Murray, London, 1956 (Wisdom of the East Series).

ARBERRY, A. J.
Sufism, George Allen & Unwin, London, 1968.

AZAD, ABUL KALAM
The Tarjuman al-Quran, Vols. 1-2, Asia Publishing House, New York, 1962.

BESANT, ANNIE
Islam, The Theosophical Publishing House, Adyar, Madras, India, 1946.

Seven Great Religions, Islam, The Theosophical Publishing House, Adyar, Madras, India, 1966.

The Universal Textbook of Religion and Morals, The Theosophical Publishing House, Adyar, Madras, India, 1962.

BHAGAVAN DAS
The Essential Unity of All Religions, The Theosophical Publishing House, Wheaton, Illinois, 1966 (Quest Book paperback).

ENCYCLOPEDIA BRITTANICA
Sufism, Vol. 21.

GABER, HOSNY M.
Outline of Islam, The Islamic Center, Washington, D. C., 1959.

GUILLAUME, ALFRED
Islam, Penguin Books, Baltimore, Maryland, 1968.

HEAD, JOSEPH, and CRANSTON, S. L.
Reincarnation, an East-West Anthology, The Theosophical Publishing House, Wheaton, Illinois, 1968 (Quest Book paperback).

LIFE EDITORIAL STAFF
The World's Great Religions, Golden Press, New York, 1967.

MORGAN, KENNETH
Islam, the Straight Path, The Ronald Press Co., New York, 1958.

POTTER, CHARLES FRANCIS
The Great Religious Leaders, Washington Square Press, New York, 1962.

RAHMAN, FAZLUR
Islam, Holt, Rinehart, and Winston, New York, 1966.

SCHUON, FRITHJOF
Understanding Islam, George Allen and Unwin, Ltd., London, 1965.

Chapter VIII

Other Living Faiths

Zoroastrianism

In man's search for truth many other religions developed over the ages in addition to the major faiths. The founders of these religions were men who had forged ahead of others on the evolutionary path. In great concern over humanity's failure to be noble and brotherly, each founder spent long periods in meditation in search for understanding of the Creator and the answers to the meaning and purpose of life.

Today these religions do not have as large followings as the major religions. Some are offshoots of other faiths. The origins of others are lost in the dim and unrecorded past. One of the oldest of these is Zoroastrianism, which some claim was contemporary with the beginnings of Hinduism.

These teachings originated in ancient Persia, now known as Iran, with early recordings dating it somewhere between 1000 and 600 B.C., although oral tradition goes back many centuries before then. Its founder was Zoroaster, or Zarathustra. There were said to be several Zarathustras before the main teacher. The last Zoroaster was born in Azerbaijan about 600 B.C. Like many other great prophets he is said to have had an unusual childhood. He had many visions. He spent twenty years in the wilderness meditating on the message he was to give humanity. When he began to teach, however, the people who had been worshiping many gods rejected his message about one God, known as *Ahura-Mazda.* Eventually the King of Persia, Vishtasp, was converted and Zoroastrianism became the religion of the country. After that it spread rapidly.

Zoroastrianism, like Hinduism, speaks of a Supreme Universal Principle which it names Ahura-Mazda. It also speaks of the triune aspect of the One Principle and a hierarchy of intelligences or gods. Fire is regarded as the supreme symbol of God. It is the symbol of divine life, and is worshiped as such by the followers of this faith. This religion teaches the concept of good and evil, and that upon the choice of man between good and evil — no matter what his creed or race may be — will depend his future life, and that he will reap the consequences of his choice. Another great concept given to the world by Zoroaster is man's function as God's co-agent in building on earth the Kingdom of Righteousness.

The teachings of Zoroaster were gathered into a scripture called *Avesta.* This gives the laws of the religion, similar to those given to the Jews in the Old Testament. This collection consisted of seventeen hymns. When the armies of Alexander the Great swept over Persia all the sacred writings were destroyed. Later King Artaxerxes revived the Zoroastrian religion in Persia and had those sacred writings that had been hidden gathered into a collection. Commentaries were added and the enlarged scriptures are called *Zend-Avesta.* This consists of hymns, prayers, myths, and religious laws.

The great virtues which the *Zend-Avesta* teaches are worship of one God, pure thought, good words, and righteous deeds.

Some of the ideas of Zoroastrianism were spread to the Jews and Muslims through trade contacts. In the earlier days the Israelites had regarded their Jehovah as a tribal God, so it seems possible that their contacts with Zoroastrians during migrations and captivity may have helped develop their ideas of God into a universal God. From them also the Jews may have taken the ideas of a judgment day. However the Zoroastrians also taught

A small Zoroastrian Temple at Adyar, Madras, India.

that by good thoughts, words, and deeds one might cancel out earlier broken laws and face a cleaner record on the final judgment day.

By the time the Muslims swept over Persia, forcing all to accept the teachings of Mohammed, the old religion had faded somewhat. The faithful ones fled to India, where they became known as the Parsis. Many of them may be found today in India and Pakistan. Quite a number live in the area around Bombay, India.

Because according to their religion the earth and the elements must be kept pure, as these are considered the pure creations of Ahura-Mazda, the Zoroastrians do not believe in burying or cremating their dead. They place the bodies on "Towers of Silence" where the vultures feed on the flesh. This custom is observed by the Parsis wherever possible and there is always a Tower of Silence in a Parsi colony.

Since the great symbol of the Zoroastrian religion is fire, which is the purifying agent, there are many prayers in this religion addressed to fire:

Happy is the man to whom thou comest nightly,
Fire, son of Ahura-Mazda. . . . O fire, son of Ahura-Mazda
We draw near to thee.*

Over the centuries a sacred fire, the symbol of truth, has been kept burning in every Zoroastrian temple. The quality of purity is much stressed in this religion, from a purity of external nature to "Pure thoughts, Pure words, Pure deeds," and the Fire is the symbol of that purity. The Parsis pray at this eternal flame, "Through the fire we draw near to thee alone, O Lord."

Their scriptures are full of moral and ethical teachings such as "Industry is better than asceticism." Another encourages brotherliness: "He who does not do his duty to those to whom duty is owed becomes a thief of duty, for he robs them of what is owing them."

Zoroastrianism, like other religions today, has lost much of its ancient fire and glory. Dr. Annie Besant, formerly president of The Theosophical Society, who understood so well the truth and beauty in all the great religions, wrote of Zoroastrianism:

* *Yasna,* xxxvi, 1,4-10

The Fire is not dead; it is only smouldering on its ancient altars; white hot are the ashes ready to reburst into flames. And I dream of the day when the breath of the great Prophet Zarathustra shall sweep again through his temples.*

Jainism

Mahavira is considered the founder of Jainism, though he had been preceded by twenty-three Jinas who taught a similar way of life. Jainism, like Buddhism, is a reform movement of Hinduism, and is practiced mostly in India. The keynote of this religion is *ahimsa,* or harmlessness. The Jains forbade the sacrifices of animals to any gods, or the taking of any form of life.

Mahavira, the teacher, was the son of the King and Queen of Magada in northern India. He was born about 600 B.C., a contemporary of Buddha. The early lives of Gautama Buddha and Mahavira are very similar. Traditions claim that Mahavira's mother also had repeated dreams when she was told she would bear a son who would become a great prophet. Miraculous events were told about his birth and early life. As a youth he lived in luxury in the royal palace. He married and had a daughter. His parents died of starvation and self-denial, as they believed that would bring them great soul progress. In grief Mahavira gave up his life of luxury, took a begging bowl and went into the silence for twelve years, seeking the cause of suffering. On attaining enlightenment, he went out to preach.

He condemned the caste system, and animal sacrifices made to the gods. He believed that men could attain Nirvana by overcoming selfish desires and by living lives of harmlessness.

This could be achieved by reincarnation and karma which are also the fundamental beliefs of the Jains. Mahavira and the twenty-three teachers who had preceded him had attained Nirvana through conquest of themselves, so were called "Conquerors."

Mahavira gave the people five rules, which are similar to five of the Ten Commandments given to Moses. They are:

Ahimsa or harmlessness. Do not kill anything, not even in defense of one's own life.
Do not lie.
Do not steal.
Live a chaste life, and do not become intoxicated.
Do not covet or desire anything for yourself.

* *Seven Great Religions,* Annie Besant

Jain Temple, Calcutta, India.

These rules had to be observed strictly by the monks, or *yatis*. These ascetics had to observe strict celibacy in compliance with the fourth command. Laymen were only expected to strive toward these ideals, which they hoped to attain fully in some later lives. The ascetic had to renounce everything and consider nothing as his own.

All Jains are vegetarians. In observance of the strict rule of *ahimsa* they must not engage in any occupation or profession that entails the taking of life. They do not fight in wars, fish, raise cattle commercially, or even farm for fear their plows will destroy some under earth creatures. As a result the Jains are merchants, manufacturers, bankers, and traders. In times of war they will only serve their country in some harmless, helpful capacity, such as to work in hospitals and in some type of clerical work.

In the Jain sacred scriptures many commands concerning *ahimsa* are similar to the following:

All living beings hate pain; therefore do not injure or kill them. This is the essence of wisdom, not to kill anything.*

So extreme are some of the monks in obeying the law of harmlessness that they wear thin masks over their mouths and noses to prevent breathing in any minute insects and destroying them. They even sweep the path in front of them while walking to avoid stepping on ants or bugs.

The Jains, like some members of other Eastern religions, teach that the main purpose of life is the evolution of the soul. Through repeated incarnations and the working of karma, man overcomes his imperfection and eventually wins freedom from physical birth. This is accomplished by harmlessness, desirelessness, right thought, and right action.

For thirty years Mahavira went about the country teaching his people. After his death, however, the Jains — as with followers of other religions — divided into sects over differing interpretations of his message.

Though Mahavira had preached against personalizing of God, it was not long after his death before his followers began carving statues of him. In time images were also made of other Jinas who had preceded him. Temples were built where worshipers paid

* *Sutra-kritange,* 1.1.9-10

homage to these teachers. Some of their finest temples in India are well known for their beautiful architecture and sculpture.

The teachings of Mahavira and the other Jinas were passed down verbally for many years. Some of these teachings were finally put into writing about the third century B.C. and are known as the *Siddhanta*. However, all the Jain teachings were not compiled until 454 A.D. The fundamentals of these teachings called "The Three Jewels" are: Right Thought, Right Knowledge, and Right Living. One of the sermons gave specific directions for freedom from earthly bondage:

> One should know what binds the soul and, knowing, break free from bondage.
> What bondage did the hero declare, and what knowledge did he teach to remove it?
> He who grasps at even a little, whether living or lifeless, or consents to another doing so, will never be free from sorrow. If a man kills living things, or slays by the hand of another, his sin goes on increasing.*

Mahavira also taught that one could not attain salvation or Nirvana through prayer, sacrifice, or worship, but only by doing good, and that "within yourself lies salvation."

The Jains have never been a proselyting or missionary sect, but are tolerant of the beliefs of others.

Shintoism

The beginning of Shintoism is lost in the vague and unrecorded past of the aborigines of the Japanese Islands. It did not develop out of the inspired teachings of one man, similar to the Buddha, Jesus Christ, or Mohammed. When the Mongolians from Asia arrived on the islands they found the people engaged in nature worship similar to their own. There were gods of the mountains, streams, rivers, forests, storms, sun, moon, and stars.

These myths of the past were finally put into writing by Yasumaro about 712 A.D. in a collection called *Kojiki* or "The Record of Ancient Things." Most of the myths were about the genealogy and activities of the gods and contained little moral and ethical teachings. This religion became known as *Shen-Teo* or Shinto meaning "the way of the gods."

* *Book of Sermons*

A Japanese family leaving a Shinto shrine.

Photograph by Harold M. Lambert

The most characteristic feature of Shintoism is the basic conviction that Gods (Kami), man, and the whole of Nature were born actually of the same parents and are therefore of the same family. Everything being Kami-born, hence everybody has a Kami-nature, and is a potential Kami (god). This belief has been the preponderant factor in the molding of the Japanese race, not only in their religious outlook but also in their social and individual pattern of behavior, in their ethical and mental attitude to life. This has given rise to a respect for and kinship with all that exists, a consciouness of unbroken continuity, a high sense of duty and a feeling of security and fearlessness — qualities which were later accentuated by Confucian and Buddhist influence.

The Sun-Goddess Amaterasu is the most important of the Shinto deities. According to the traditions the emperors had sprung from her, and were considered divine. After Japan's defeat at the end of World War II in 1947, Emperor Hirohita announced that he was a mere man and not divine. Since then Shintoism has no longer been the state religion of Japan.

Buddhist missionaries reached Japan in the sixth century A.D. Prince Shotoku became interested in Buddhism and consulted the Sun Goddess about it. She approved, saying the Buddhas were from the same source as their gods. So many of the teachings of the Buddha were incorporated into Shintoism. Confucianism, with its ancestor worship, also helped shape the beliefs and ceremonies of Shintoism. The people were taught that the Buddha and Bodhisattvas were similar to their own *Kami,* or gods. Thus Shinto became so tolerant of other beliefs that one could be a Buddhist and also worship in the Shinto shrines.

There are over a hundred thousand shrines scattered over the islands. Most of these are of unpainted wood and so perishable they have to be rebuilt every few years. The most famous of the shrines is the Imperial Shrine, which is in the Ise-Shima National Park in South Honshu, Japan. This shrine was always visited by the emperor soon after ascending the throne. Many Shinto worshipers make pilgrimages to the Imperial Shrine, just as Muslims go to Mecca, and Christians and Jews to Jerusalem and Bethlehem.

One of the ceremonies performed at the shrines twice a year is the ritual of purification. Before attending the service everyone bathes and abstains from food. The priest conducts the service and accepts the penalty offerings. Each person has a paper effigy of himself, which he rubs over his body to transfer his sins to the effigy. Later the priest collects these and throws them into the sea or a stream to be washed clean. This ceremony takes place at a specific time in all the shrines of Japan.

This is symbolic and may be compared somewhat with the Christian ceremony of baptism by water in which the person is washed of his sins to begin a new life. The Hindus and Buddhists observe a similar ritual by bathing in the sacred river Ganga or in any other sacred waters.

People go to Shinto shrines daily to pray for abundance of harvest, for luck with their fishing fleets, and forgiveness of sins and for aid in all their endeavors. Their religion has no definite commandments. From Buddhism they have learned the laws of karma, that there is painful reaction from all broken laws of nature. There are no scriptures similar to the high spiritual teachings given by other religions. However, their books of poems and prayers have inculcated in the Japanese people a fine ethical code, which condemns many evils such as adultery, lying, cowardice, stealing, and witchcraft.

A Collection of Myriad Leaves contains over four hundred poems expressing the love of nature and of the inspiring Japanese landscape. Their paintings also have a delicate quality, revealing the artists' love of the beautiful. The *Yengihiki* is filled with prayers asking for forgiveness of sins. Some authors have compiled prayers taken from the walls of the shrines, such as this one:

> Listen all ye who come before me in the hope of attaining your desires. Pray with hearts pure from all untruth, and hearts clean wherein Truth can be seen as in a mirror.

Though the Shinto religion has honored many gods, including the emperors, some verses and quotations on the walls of the shrines encourage a search for the divine in every human soul. For example:

> The first and surest means to enter into communion with the divine is by sincerity. If you pray with sincerity, you will feel the divine presence.

The *Bushido* code shapes the conduct of the Shinto warriors, and is an ideal for Japanese laymen as well. There are eight virtues for which they must strive: loyalty, gratitude, courage, justice, truthfulness, politeness, reserve, and honor.

The center of worship in the Japanese home is the god-shelf, or *Kami-dana*. This shelf generally contains tablets of the family's favorite god and some honored ancestors. At this family altar a brief prayer is said daily, or an offering made of food or flowers.

Shintoism, like other religions, is now divided into many sects. Since the separation of state and church these sects have increased to about 800. Shintoism now has approximately 35,000,000 followers among the various sects.

Sikhism

Sikhism developed in the Punjab area of northern India in the fifteenth century A.D. The founder of this religion was Nanak, who was born near Lahore in 1469 of devout Hindu parents. He tried to harmonize the beliefs of the Hindus and the Muslims. Nanak was followed by nine other teachers, or gurus.

The teachings given out by Nanak and the nine gurus who followed him are believed to be divinely inspired. Nanak, like other great teachers, spent long periods alone in meditation and a search for truth before bringing his message to the people. He discarded the prevailing Hindu idea of many gods (although in Hinduism there is also the concept of the existence of the One Supreme Principle, eternal, all-pervading) and accepted the Islamic teaching of one God, whom he called Sat-Nam, which when translated means the True Name. He did not approve of many rituals and ceremonies, claiming they prevented true contemplation.

Nanak was a natural poet, so that his teachings were expressed through hymns and verses. There are 974 of these poems which were memorized by his disciples and passed down from generation to generation. The fifth guru, Arjan, finally had them written in a Punjabi dialect and called it the *Adi-Granth* which is considered the sacred scriptures of the Sikhs. Over 200 of Arjan's verses were also included. Many are similar to the teachings of Hinduism and Islam. The Sikhs teach that God has sent other messengers to various people from time to time and that instructions had also been given them for freedom from the round of rebirths.

Sikhism teaches that the karmic bondages could be erased

The Golden Temple, the most sacred shrine of the Sikhs, Amritsar, North India.

here in this one human life by the Grace of one Personal-Absolute God which is to be invoked not merely through way of work, or way of knowledge, but by dwelling upon and following the Way of the Name (Nam-marg). It is not through renunciation but by participating in the activity of life in a detached manner without getting involved in it, that one follows the *Nam-marg*.

Nanak taught his pupils to begin every day with the recitation of some sacred scripture, followed by meditation. One of the hymns which most Sikhs repeat daily begins:

> There is one God,
> Eternal Truth is His Name.
> Maker of all things
> Fearing nothing and at enmity with nothing,
> Timeless is his image;
> Not begotten, being of his own Being;
> By the grace of our Guru made known to man.

Many of Nanak's verses have been set to music and are sung regularly in the temples. Traditions claim that Nanak visited the Islamic shrine in Mecca and the Hindu Temple of Krishna in Puri. He did not approve of the caste system. He said a man could serve best in his own home and chosen work.

Both Muslims and Hindus resisted the new religion, forcing the Sikhs to fight for their faith. They were conquered and persecuted by Muslims who over-ran and occupied their territory around Lahore. Eventually the Sikhs, led by Govind Singh, brought Lahore and the surrounding territory under their own control again.

Govind Singh, who was born in 1675, became the tenth guru of the Sikhs. He introduced a more militant teaching. He wrote "I bow to Him who holdeth the arrow in one hand. I bow to the Fearless One."

He organized a militant group, initiating the members with a special form of baptism, and called them *Lions*. They were trained to fight for their faith against Muslims, Hindus, and the British. Their war cry was, "The pure are of God, and the victory is to God."

Sikhs are easily recognized by their long hair and beards, steel bracelets, and turbans.

The teachings of Govind Singh were eventually compiled into

a new scripture called *The Granth of the Tenth Guru*. This became part of the Sikh scriptures along with the earlier *Adi-Granth*.

After the ten gurus were gone the *Guru-Granth* was regarded as the teacher. During his lifetime Arjan had completed the famous Golden Temple at Amritsar in the Punjab, surrounded by a moat or lake. The *Guru-Granth* is placed under a jeweled canopy in a Sikh temple and read aloud. The verses are also sung in the temples.

All through these scriptures flows great reverence for the Creator:

> In every way I said, there is no other, O friend
> He dwells in all the continents and islands
> He fills all Lokas (places).[1]

Their teachings about karma are similar to the Hindu ideas:

> On karma the teaching is clear;
> Soweth himself, eateth himself.[2]

Though the Sikhs rejected the discrimination caused by the caste system, they teach that the station of man's birth is controlled by actions in his previous lives:

> According to one's action are caste and birth. . . .[3]

The instructions on self-discipline were emphasized by all the gurus:

> Without practicing virtues, devotion is not possible.[4]

> Of the things to be renounced, the most to be recommended are lust, hatred and avarice.

> Hear thou! Meditating on Hari's name do charity to all.[5]

Though there are today about 6,000,000 Sikhs living mainly in the Punjab area of India, little is known about them in the West, except for the valor of their warrior Lions.

Baha'i Faith

The Shi'ites of Persia believed another prophet was to follow Mohammed. In 1844 Mirza Ali Muhammed rebelled against the old teachings and announced himself as the forerunner of the

[1] Guru V, Devgandhari
[2] Guru I, Japaji
[3] Guru 1, Prabhati
[4] Guru I, Japaji
[5] Guru V, Majh

The Baha'i House of Worship, Wilmette, Illinois.

Photograph by Harold M. Lambert

new prophet who was expected. This was to be a teacher to establish a new religion and a new world order for all men. Mirza Ali Muhammed became known as "the Bab," or Gate. Many followers accepted his message. However, when the new movement grew and seemed to threaten the ruling powers of Persia, the Bab and 20,000 of his followers were put to death.

In 1863 Baha'u'llah — a name which means "the glory of God" — was declared to be the expected teacher. He was soon exiled to Bagdad where he gained many followers there and in other cities of Asia Minor. He was imprisoned many times for his ideas until finally the Turks imprisoned him in Palestine where he spent the rest of his life and died in 1892. He had appointed his son, Abdul'l-Baha, to be Guardian of the Faith after his death. Abdul'l-Baha continued his teaching, writing, and missionary work until his death in 1921, when Shohgi Effendi continued his work.

These four teachers have left a large amount of literature on the Baha'i Faith. The main purpose of these teachings is to unify the world into a world brotherhood under one faith to pave the way for world peace. Their literature gives specific instructions for the formation of this world order. Baha'u'llah wrote "The earth is but one country, and mankind the citizens. . . . Ye are the fruits of one tree and the leaves of one branch."

The Baha'is teach that other prophets have brought divine revelations to suit men's needs at various stages of their development, recognizing the valuable teachings of such inspired ones as Krishna, the Buddha, Confucius, Moses, Jesus Christ, and others. However, they teach that Baha'u'llah and his followers have come with a new message for humanity to unite the world in one religious and political body. Preparations for this new world order must be made through universal education, and a common language for all people, to promote mutual understanding. They advocate a Parliament of Nations to settle world questions.

The Baha'i teachings explain that there are cycles of a thousand years each in the progress of humanity and that the Baha'i faith is the message for this age. Their scriptures state: "That which the Lord hath ordained as the sovereign remedy for the healing of all the world is the union of its people in one Universal Cause, one Common Faith."

God can be known only through his prophets, they maintain.

The Baha'i goal, as in many other faiths, is the attaining of human perfection. Baha'u'llah described in *The Seven Valleys* the paths men must cross in climbing toward that height: search, love, divine unity, contentment, astonishment, poverty, and annihilation. In the end each soul must gain all the virtues of a superman when he may say with the Christians and others, "Not my will but Thine be done."

The Baha'i teachings have been translated into about 400 languages and dialects. Groups have been organized in practically every country of the world. The new faith is receiving an especially warm welcome in Africa. In the United States there are over 200 centers. The governing body is called the National Spiritual Assembly. In 1970 there were approximately 35,000 Baha'is in the United States and an estimate of 5,000,000 in the entire world.

World headquarters for the Baha'i Faith is at Haifa, Israel. The headquarters in the United States is at Wilmette, Illinois, where a beautiful nine-sided temple has been erected. The Nine sides symbolize the nine great world religions, with doors open to people of all faiths. Temples of similar design have been built in other countries as well.

Suggested Further Reading:

Zoroastrianism

BESANT, ANNIE
Seven Great Religions, Zoroastrianism, The Theosophical Publishing House, Adyar, Madras, India, 1966.

BODE, F. A., and NANAVUTTY, P.
Songs of Zarathushtra, George Allen & Unwin, London, 1952.

DAWSON, MILES
Ethical Religion of Zoroaster, Macmillan & Co., New York, 1931.

MASANI, RUSTOM
Zoroastrianism, Macmillan & Co., New York, 1968.

RUSTOMJEE, F.
Catechism of the Teachings of Holy Zarathustra, D. B. Taraparevala Sons & Co., Private Ltd., Bombay, India.

Shintoism

BRUCE, W. K.
Religions in Japan, Charles E. Tuttle & Co., Rutland, Vermont, 1967.

FRAZIER, ALLIE M.
Readings in Eastern Religious Thought: Chinese and Japanese Religions, Westminster Press, Philadelphia, Pa., 1967.

HERBERT, JEAN
Shinto, George Allen & Unwin, Ltd., London, 1967.

ONO, SOKYO
Shinto: The Kami Way, Charles E. Tuttle & Co., Rutland, Vt., 1969.

TSUNDA, RYUSAKU, DE BARRY, WM. THEODORE, and KEENE, DONALD
Sources of Japanese Tradition, Vols. 1-2, Columbia University Press, New York, 1968.

Sikhism

BESANT, ANNIE
Seven Great Religions, Sikhism, The Theosophical Publishing House, Adyar, Madras, India, 1966.

FIELD, DOROTHY
The Religion of the Sikhs, Dutton & Co., New York, 1914 (Wisdom of the East Series).

SINGH, TRILACHAN and Others
Sacred Writings of the Sikhs, George Allen & Unwin, London, 1965.

Jainism

BESANT, ANNIE
Seven Great Religions, Jainism, The Theosophical Publishing House, Adyar, Madras, India, 1966.

BHARGAVA, D.
Jaina Ethics, Motilal Banarsidass, Delhi, India, 1968.

DE BARRY, WM. THEODORE
Sources of Indian Tradition, Vol. 1, Columbia University Press, New York, 1967.

SCHUBRING, WALTHER
The Doctrine of the Jainas, Motilal Banarsidass, Delhi, India, 1968.

Religion of the Jainas, Motilal Banarsidass, Delhi, India, 1966.

Baha'i

BAHA'I PUBLISHING COMMITTEE
Baha'i World Faith, Wilmette, Illinois, 1943.

ESSELEMONT, J. E.
Baha'u'llah and The New Era, Baha'i Publishing Trust, Wilmette, Illinois, 1940.

SHOGHI, EFFENDI
Gleanings from the Writings of Baha'u'llah, Baha'i Publishing Trust, Wilmette, Illinois, 1963.

The World Order of Baha'u'llah, Baha'i Publishing Trust, Wilmette, Illinois, 1955.

TOWNSHEND, GEORGE
The Glad Tidings of Baha'u'llah, John Murray, London, 1949 (Wisdom of the East Series).

Chapter IX

New Horizons

As man has climbed out of the dark valley of ignorance toward the mountain peak of oneness with God, his horizon has broadened. His concepts have changed from tribal gods, which he encased in wood, stone, and gold, to a Creator whose infinite glory cannot be bound by the farthest star. The cry in the 1960s was that "God is dead." But it is not new, for man has been creating gods in his own image since the dawn of spiritual awareness and, as time has passed, he has destroyed the old images when newer vistas opened to him on the ascending path of evolutionary development.

The religious paths man has followed have been many, but each has provided lessons needed for spiritual growth. After the passing of the founders and their closest disciples, each of the religions lost some of its pristine glory, as it became divided into sects and denominations, with varying interpretations of the scriptures. This created bigotry, prejudice, and even wars, separating the followers of the teachers from one another.

In age after age, when the religion fell into malpractices, a new teacher came to give a fresh impetus to man's spiritual development, bringing new forms designed to develop different facets of universal truths. Now, in the twentieth century when science and technology are shrinking space and bringing people closer together, a new light is dawning. It was a significant moment when the three astronauts, Major William C. Anders, Captain James Lovell, and Colonel Frank Borman on Christmas Eve (1968) telecast, read from outer space while looking back on the earth:

> In the beginning God created the heaven and the earth . . .
> And God said, Let there be light; and there was light.[1]

The light of truth has been there all along at the core of all the living religions, but man has so encased it in walls of ritual, dogma, and creed, that the real meaning has often been hard to find. Many people are prone to condemn a religion because some of its followers fail to live up to the high ideals of the true teachings. Few Christians are able to become "a perfect man, unto the measure of the stature of the fullness of Christ." [2] So none should sit in judgment on those of other religions who fail to attain the ideals set by their teachers. In the Orient the spiritual foundations were laid, out of which other faiths have evolved. In studying these many religions and searching for their meanings, we discover two fundamental truths running through them all: the spiritual source of all life and the Brotherhood of Man.

In recent years steps have been taken to harmonize the conflicting elements of the many religions of the world. One of the earliest of these organizations is The Theosophical Society founded in 1875 by a Russian woman, Helena Petrovna Blavatsky, and an American, Colonel Henry Steel Olcott, who organized the Society in New York City. The organization became world-wide and its headquarters was established eventually at Adyar, Madras, India. Each year conferences are held there, attended by representatives of all the religions and people from many countries of the world. There are branches of the Society in more than 60 countries of the world. Its main object is to "form a nucleus of the universal brotherhood of humanity, without distinction of race, creed, sex, caste, or color."

[1] Genesis 1:1,3
[2] Ephesians 4:13

To put these ideals into practice has been difficult in a world torn by religious prejudice and racial hatred. Even today, a century after the founding of the movement, the struggle has just reached the catalytic stage, out of which should come tolerance, harmony, and world peace. The expression, "without distinction of race, creed, sex, caste, or color" is now heard in many tongues and is the banner waved by many groups now seeking the same goal.

The United Nations, though primarily a political organization, is contributing something toward understanding other people. The Ecumenical Movement is trying to bring the separated branches of the Christian religion, Protestant and Catholics and Jews into harmonious relationship. This is a great step in the right direction, but it has not gone far enough to include the Far Eastern religions also.

The World Council of Churches, which meets at Geneva, Switzerland, with representatives from 90 countries and 214 denominations of the Protestant Christian faith, is trying to harmonize the conflicting interpretations of their faith and find a common basis for working together.

Other movements have a broader scope in the direction of true brotherhood of humanity, for they include the living religions of all the world. A Spiritual Summit Conference was held in Calcutta in 1968 to discuss the goals of common belief and common brotherhood. This was held under the auspices of the Temple of Understanding, which was organized by Mrs. Dickerman Hollister in America. Attending this gathering were representatives of Christianity, Buddhism, Hinduism, Islam, Judaism. Confucianism, Zoroastrianism, Jainism, Sikhism, and the Baha'i Faith.

Another movement working for the cause of brotherhood. tolerance, and understanding among various religious groups, is the Spiritual Unity of Nations, founded by Joseph Busby of Sussex. England. Its aim is "To mobilize the spiritual powers of the world religions and other spiritual movements and within the hearts of people of the world, for bringing about a World Spiritual Unity of Nations."

These and other great movements are doing much to bring people into harmony and to overcome prejudices and racial hatreds. A blind poet, the Reverend G. Matheson, expressed this ideal beautifully:

Gather us in, we worship only Thee:
In varied names we stretch a common hand;
In diverse forms a common soul we see;
In many ships we seek a promised land.

Thine is the mystic life great India craves,
Thine is the Parsi's purifying beam.
Thine the Buddhist's rest from tossing waves,
Thine is the Empire of vast China's dream.

Some seek a father in the Heaven above;
Some ask a human image to adore;
Some crave a spirit vast as life and love;
Within thy mansions we have all and more.

O glorious Triune God, embracing all,
By many paths do we approach Thy throne;
All paths are Thine; Thou hearest every call,
Each earnest seeker has Thee for his own.

Suggested Further Reading:

General

BESANT, ANNIE
Seven Great Religions, The Theosophical Publishing House, Adyar, Madras, India, 1966.

BROWNE, LEWIS
This Believing World, The Macmillan Co., New York, 1928.

BHAGAVAN DAS
The Essential Unity of All Religions, The Theosophical Publishing House, Wheaton, Illinois, 1966 (Quest Book paperback).

FRAZER, JAMES GEORGE
The Golden Bough, 8 vols., St. Martin's Press, New York, 1963.

GAER, JOSEPH
What the Great Religions Believe, Dodd, Mead & Co., 1963.

Wisdom of the Living Religions, Dodd, Mead & Co., 1956.

HUXLEY, ALDOUS
The Perennial Philosophy, Harper & Bros., New York, 1945.

JAMES, E. G.
History of Religions, Harper, New York, 1957.

LANDIS, BENSON Y.
World Religions, E. P. Dutton & Co., New York, 1957.

LIFE EDITORIAL STAFF
The World's Great Religions, Golden Press, New York, 1967.

NOSS, JOHN B.
Man's Religions, The Macmillan Co., New York, 1963.

PARRINDER, E. G.
A Book of World Religions, Dufour Editions, Inc., Chester Springs, Penna., 1967.

Index